THE VICTORIA HISTORY OF LEICESTERSHIRE

CASTLE DONINGTON

Pamela J. Fisher and J.M. Lee

First published 2016

A Victoria County History publication

© The University of London, 2016

ISBN 978 1 909646 27 8

Cover image: View of central Castle Donington, looking north-west from a path near the airport boundary.
Back cover image: The river Trent and converted workers' cottages at King's Mills, from Weston-on-Trent parish.

Typeset in Minion pro by Emily Morrell

CONTENTS

LIST OF ILLUSTRATIONS

We are grateful to The Record Office for Leicestershire, Leicester and Rutland (figures 6, 7, 8), Castle Donington Museum (figures 2, 9, 12, 14), Derby Museums (figure 1) and Geoff Shaw (figure 10) for permission to publish these images. The photograph on the front cover is by Jane Rennie, and all other photographs are by Pamela Fisher.

Map

FOREWORD

As PRESIDENT OF THE LEICESTERSHIRE Victoria County History Trust I am delighted that this book covering the parish of Castle Donington is now published, being the first of what will be a growing series of publications covering the county of Leicestershire. This work is being published by the Victoria County History, a national organisation based in the University of London, which ensures that the series of publications throughout England achieves a consistent high standard. The books are distributed throughout this country and abroad.

The Victoria County History began in 1899 when it was dedicated to Queen Victoria, and ever since has been working to write the history of every village and town in England. In 2012 the Victoria County History was rededicated to Queen Elizabeth II, in celebration of Her Majesty's Diamond Jubilee, and so renewed the royal connection with this great enterprise.

In Leicestershire four successful Victoria County History volumes known as the 'red books' were published between 1950 and 1965, but until recently it has not proved possible to make further progress; and so this book on Castle Donington is a very welcome addition to the history of Leicestershire, and along with further publications will in due course be included in future red book volumes.

The original work, which was produced by Michael Lee, has been greatly expanded and brought up to date by Pam Fisher with the help of local volunteers and Delia Richards in particular. Readers will appreciate the energy and expertise that Pam has put into the project, and she deserves all our thanks for bringing the work to a successful conclusion.

This book will appeal, of course, to the residents of Castle Donington but the story that is told and the history that is recorded in this book will have a wider appeal to all those who have an interest in the history of our rich and diverse county, and I commend it to you.

Jennifer, Lady Gretton JP
HM Lord-Lieutenant of Leicestershire

ACKNOWLEDGEMENTS

THIS IS A BOOK WITH A HISTORY of its own. Its genesis lies in a history of Castle Donington parish written by Michael Lee for Leicestershire Victoria County History in *c.*1954, when a lack of funds prevented its publication. Castle Donington has changed significantly since the 1950s, and additional material has been added by Pam Fisher to bring the history up to date, including new research on earlier periods, where improved cataloguing and digital technology has made many sources more accessible.

The authors are very grateful for the support and encouragement provided in the 1950s by the late W.G. Hoskins, the late Jack Simmons and former county archivist L.A. Parker. We are pleased that this research can now reach a wider audience, for which thanks are due to Christopher Dyer, who has been unfailingly generous with advice, support and encouragement, to Delia Richards, whose local knowledge, assistance and enthusiasm has been invaluable, and to John Beckett, who introduced the two authors to each other in 2010, providing the initial impetus for this publication.

We are also very grateful to Castle Donington Parish Council, the Duchy of Lancaster Benevolent Fund and to the Victoria County History Trust for their kind and generous grants, and to Leicestershire Victoria County History Trust's many donors and supporters, without whom this publication could not have been completed.

Many other people have contributed in different ways, and we thank Martyn Bennett, Anne Bryan, Carol Cambers, Patrick Clay, Mandy DeBelin, Helen Edwards, Robert Hartley, Andrew Hopper, Susan Kilby, Jane Laughton, Peter Liddle, Hazel Pearson, Jane Rennie, John Shields, Anthony Squires, Joanna Story, Matt Tomkins, Bruce Townsend, Carol Walton and Eric Wheeler, who have kindly shared with us their specialist knowledge and skills. Others have provided information or made documents available to us, both in the 1950s and more recently, and their help is acknowledged within the footnotes.

Archivists, librarians and staff have been consistently helpful at the Record Office for Leicestershire, Leicester and Rutland, The National Archives, BT Archives, the Church of England Records Centre, the David Wilson Library at the University of Leicester, Derbyshire Local Studies Library, Derbyshire Museums, Derbyshire Record Office, HSBC Archives, the Huntington Library in San Marino, Lambeth Palace Library, Leicestershire County Council Historic and Natural Environment team, Lincolnshire Archives, Northamptonshire Record Office, Nottinghamshire Archives and the Post Office Archives. Special thanks are also due to Lord Ralph Kerr for allowing us to consult the extensive Melbourne Hall archive, and to Estate archivist Philip Heath.

Publication would not have been possible without the support of the staff at VCH Central Office, especially Richard Hoyle, Adam Chapman and Jessica Davies, and their anonymous reviewers who commented helpfully on an earlier version of this text: we thank them all. We are also very grateful to the President of Leicestershire Victoria County History Trust, Jennifer, Lady Gretton, for contributing the foreword.

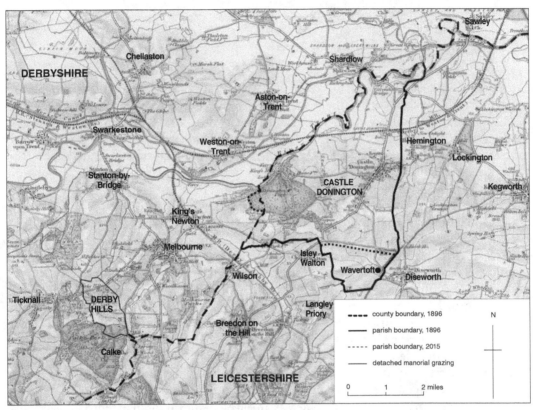

Map 1 *The parish of Castle Donington in 1896, showing relief, the detached portion of the manor at Derby Hills and places mentioned in the text.*

CASTLE DONINGTON, IN NORTH-WEST LEICESTERSHIRE, stands in the heart of the East Midlands, 20 miles north-west of Leicester, 8 miles south-east of Derby and 13 miles south-west of Nottingham. East Midlands Airport lies in the south of the parish, and the River Trent forms the northern and western boundaries; this stretch of the river is also the county boundary between Leicestershire and Derbyshire. Castle Donington developed several features of a town in the Middle Ages, including a market and fair granted in 1278, but wears its history lightly. The remains of the castle and medieval hospital are largely hidden from view, and Donington Park, which attracts many visitors annually for motor-racing and festivals, is not generally recognised as a medieval hunting park.

Most residents in 2016 do not consider Castle Donington to be a town, but neither is it a typical village. The name, width and continuous frontages of Borough Street (the main shopping area) suggest a place of some importance, and the independence of spirit evident from the building of multiple places of worship, and the size and architecture of the Edwardian school building are urban in character, albeit on a small scale. Donington has also sustained a range of trades over many centuries, with the 21st century seeing accountancy, hospitality, warehousing and distribution replacing agriculture, basket-making, lace and hosiery, as the availability of land and excellent road and air connections have attracted businesses.

Parish Boundaries

The parish contained 1,385 ha. (3,422 a.) in 2011, and was almost triangular in shape.[1] From its south-western corner, the boundary (also the county boundary with Derbyshire at this point) took an almost straight line north-eastwards for 0.8 miles to meet the earthworks of a medieval park pale. Extending north from this point, these earthworks formerly marked the parish and county boundaries, but the park was extended westwards, probably in the 17th century,[2] and the administrative boundaries were altered in 1965 to follow the new park boundary to the River Trent, transferring 15 a. from Melbourne and Derbyshire to Castle Donington and Leicestershire (Map 1).[3]

The ancient parish and county boundaries crossed the river and followed its northern bank, in line with a settlement agreed between the earl of Lincoln and the abbot of Chester in 1310, giving the earl (the lord of Donington), the whole of the river with its valuable fishing rights, 'as his ancestors have been accustomed'.[4] The boundary was moved to the centre of the Trent in 1991, in line with the usual custom, except for a small deviation near King's Mills,[5] crossing to the south bank almost midway between the road crossings at Cavendish Bridge and Sawley, at the site of a succession of medieval bridges. Moving south-east for a short distance along a paleo-channel of the river, the parish boundary then doubled back on itself for 0.6 miles along a sinuous bank and ditch, embracing within the parish a possible early medieval watermill and series of fish weirs.[6] This earthwork (Tipnall Bank) is named in an account roll of 1421, when it was said to contain 2 a.,[7] and may not be much older, as an early medieval ditch extends beneath it at one point.[8] The boundary then turned sharply south, following a sinuous water course for 0.4 miles, then a drainage ditch and low bank which runs almost due south for one mile, to reach the foot of the sandstone ridge on which the village sits. A map of Hemington from 1740 shows that this part of the boundary was just as straight before the

1   2011 census.
2   Below, 34–5.
3   http://www.visionofbritain.org.uk/unit/10372690 (accessed 13 Jul. 2013).
4   *Cart. Chester*, II, 475–7.
5   Boundary Commission, Rpt no. 577 (1989), 6; Derb., Leics., Lincs., Notts. and Warws. (County Boundaries) Order, 1991.
6   Cooper and Ripper , 11.
7   TNA, DL 29/183/2903, rot. 2.
8   Cooper and Ripper , 37. This ditch meets the bank at SK 454298.

inclosure of either village,[9] but no evidence reveals when this water-course was dug or straightened.

The boundary continued south over rising ground for a further 1.6 miles, skirting former open field furlongs before crossing the airport to reach a point just to the south of Ashby Road (designated A453 in 2015). Before 1936, the boundary ran south-west from this point, but in that year 414 a. was transferred from Castle Donington to form part of a new civil parish of Isley-cum-Langley.[10] A new boundary was drawn which ran west for 1.4 miles, parallel to and a short distance south of the road, then crossed the road to reach Donington Park. It then picked up the fossilized edges of the furlongs of a former open field for 0.5 miles, to reach the south-west tip of the parish and the Derbyshire boundary already mentioned.

Before 1936, from the point to the south of the Ashby Road, the boundary ran south-west for 0.7 miles, initially along a green lane, before making a slight detour to the east at Diseworth Brook. It then ran west for a further 0.7 miles, encompassing the former monastic estate of Wavertoft, dividing this from the lands of Langley priory, immediately to the south. Turning north, it made two large dog-legs to reach a point near the junction of the A453 trunk route with the main north-south road through Castle Donington, where it continued as indicated above.

A detached portion of the manor known as Derby Hills, 5 miles south-west of the village centre and wholly within Derbyshire, provided c.300 a. of upland wood pasture,[11] with a small stream running west-east through the centre. A plan of this hilly area in 1723 shows it was surrounded by Calke Mill (to the south-east), Calke Park and inclosures, and the commons of the Derbyshire villages of Calke, Ticknall, Stanton-by-Bridge and Melbourne. Most of this land was common pasture before inclosure in 1770,[12] with grazing rights held by Donington's copyholders.[13] Part of the area was subsequently flooded by the creation of Staunton Harold reservoir, which opened in 1965.[14]

Landscape and Geology

A prominent ridge of sandstone of the Bromsgrove formation runs almost due east-west across the centre of the parish. Its northern edge falls away sharply to a low-lying plain along Spittal [road], and also forms part of the castle defences. The southern edge of this ridge is less well defined, fading away south of Park Lane, with smaller sandstone deposits around Hill Top, near the northern boundary of the airport.[15] Two steep-sided valleys cut through the ridge: Stud Brook runs north through the westernmost valley, while the eastern valley, which is also the main road through the village, carries the waters of the culverted town brook northwards. There is a spring on the land of the former medieval hospital.

9   ROLLR, Misc 533.
10   http://www.visionofbritain.org.uk/unit/10372690 (accessed 22 Mar. 2016).
11   Melb. Hall Est. Office, X94/P 1/12; Derb. RO, Q/RI 34 (quoting different acreages).
12   Melb. Hall Est. Office, X94/P/1/12; 10 Geo. III, c. 13; Derb. RO, Q/RI 34.
13   ROLLR, DG 8/3, 4, 11, 15, 16, 22, 31.
14   ROLLR, 32D 73/809.
15   http://mapapps.bgs.ac.uk/geologyofbritain/home.html (accessed 11 Feb. 2016).

The low-lying northern plain contains *c*.405 ha. (*c*.1,000 a.) of land, 29 per cent of the modern parish, and is *c*.30 m. above sea level. It is bounded by the river Trent, which meanders slowly north-eastwards, and is prone to changing its course as sediment is deposited. The bedrock is Mercia mudstone, mostly of the Edwalton member, topped with silt, gravel and a mixed alluvium. There are a small number of gravel pits to the north-east, but in 2015 most of the local gravel extraction had been in Lockington cum Hemington parish, and north of the river, in Derbyshire. Research into the changing nature of the Trent in this area suggests a progression from a wandering gravel-bed river in the 8th and 9th centuries, to a braided formation with several channels and islands between the 10th and 12th centuries, with these channels gradually joining between the 12th and 17th centuries to create a single meandering course.[16] Watery paleochannels can be seen in several places.

There are several documentary references to the changing river course. The lord of Weston-on-Trent in *c*.1171–90 gave to the lord of Donington land in Weston which the river had separated from the rest of Weston manor;[17] in 1310 it was agreed that Donington's lord would provide a road through his meadow and pasture called Langholm to enable hay and grass from the lord of Weston's meadow called le Steure to be taken across the river;[18] and in the 1660s, Donington manor received 8*d.* annually from the inhabitants of Wilne and Shardlow for access to their 'Misbegotten meadow'.[19] Donington's inclosure award of 1779 includes an allotment of meadow to the rector of Aston in lieu of tithes on former 'Aston' land, and osiers on Aston's side of the river were within Donington's bounds.[20] There was some building on this plain after the railway opened in 1869, but most development has been since the Second World War, notably the power station, which opened in 1958 (later demolished), and the creation since the early 1970s of Trent Lane Industrial Estate and Willow Farm Business Park.

The houses and farms of the village are on the eastern half of the sandstone ridge, and almost extend to the parish boundary. This land is 60–80 m. above sea level, and the topsoil is largely loam. The western half of this ridge is farmland, encroached upon by housebuilding. The extreme western edge is wooded, and drops sharply to the river at King's Mills. Part of this land was known in the 14th century as 'Le Milneclif',[21] and its 'bold projecting crag, with hanging woods' attracted artists of the Picturesque movement in the 18th century (Fig. 1).[22] Trees continued to hug the top of the 'cliff' in 2015, which, at its steepest point north-west of Donington Hall, is almost vertical.

South of the sandstone ridge, the bedrock is Tarporley siltstone formation, mostly covered by clay. Donington Hall, its park, woods, motor-racing circuit and farmland are to the west, where the land rises to peaks *c*.100 m. above sea level. To the east of Stud Brook the land is also 80–100 m. above sea level. Much of the former farmland here

---

16   A.G. Brown, 'The geomorphology and environment of the Hemington reach', in Ripper and Cooper, 158.

17   *Cart. Chester*, I, 214.

18   *Cart. Chester* II, 475–7.

19   Town bk, 1661.

20   ROLLR, DE 5251/1.

21   *Cal. Close*, 1330–33, 212.

22   J. Britton, *The Beauties of England and Wales*, IX (1807), 402; engraving held by Derby Museum. A slightly different version of Figure 1 is within the 'Grangerised' Nichols, held at ROLLR.

Figure 1 *King's Mills: an engraving of 1745 by François Vivares from a painting by Thomas Smith of Derby.*

has been taken for the airport, hotels, businesses and housing. One of the former open fields of the parish, and the former grange and its closes at Wavertoft, extended south of the modern parish boundary, where the land falls gradually to the Diseworth Brook, a tributary of the River Soar.

Communication

River and canal

The Trent has been used to transport goods for thousands of years. Two log boats, one radiocarbon dated to 1440–1310 BC and both carrying blocks of local Bromsgrove sandstone have been found in the parishes of Aston-on-Trent and Shardlow.[23]

By the Middle Ages, the changing course of the river, the deposition of silt and the erection of weirs and water mills impeded long journeys. The head of navigation until 1699 was generally recognised as Nottingham, several miles downriver to the east,[24] but the upper reaches of the Trent at least as far as Donington were accessible by some vessels.[25] A proposal to extend the navigation from Castle Donington at Wilden Ferry to Burton-upon-Trent (Staffs.) was rejected in 1665,[26] but a later attempt by Lord Paget of

---

23 D. Knight and A.J. Howard, 'From Neolithic to early Bronze Age: the first agricultural landscapes', in D. Knight and A.J. Howard (eds.), *Trent Valley Landscapes* (King's Lynn, 2004), 58–9.
24 C.C. Owen, 'The early history of the upper Trent navigation', *Transport History*, I (1968), 235.
25 *HMC, Cowper II*, 306.
26 *VCH Staffs.*, IX, 27.

Burton received parliamentary assent in 1699.[27] George Hayne of Wirksworth (Derb.) leased the navigation from Paget for 31 years from 1711,[28] and went into partnership with Leonard Fosbrooke of Wilden Ferry.[29] The Act enabled Hayne and Fosbrooke to prevent others operating wharves or warehouses between Nottingham and Burton, giving them a monopoly.[30] It was alleged they took eight times the permitted 3*d.* per ton through wharfage charges,[31] destroyed a new house to prevent it being used as a warehouse, prevented entry to a lock and blocked the river, first by a ferry rope and then by a chain of boats.[32] Despite this, their lease was extended for a further 20 years in 1742.[33] In 1749 they allegedly sank a barge in King's Mills lock, forcing trans-shipment around it for eight years.[34] Their lease was not renewed again.

Natural impediments between Wilden Ferry and Burton included many 'shoals and scours'. In dry seasons the water was only eight inches deep in places,[35] but in winter the river tended to flood. In 1766 a bill was placed before parliament, supported by merchants and traders in Staffordshire and London, for a canal to be cut from 'near Wilden Ferry' to the river Mersey.[36] The southern part of this canal (the Grand Trunk) opened to Shugborough (Staffs.) in 1770;[37] it was completed to the Mersey in 1777,[38] and became known as the Trent and Mersey canal. It joins the Trent at the river's confluence with the river Derwent, downriver from Donington, effectively turning the river alongside Donington into a backwater.[39] The Trent navigation ceased in 1805, when the lessee reached an agreement with the canal's largest carrier.[40]

Fords and Ferries for Derby

There was a ford in Donington in 1310 near meadow and pasture called Langholm, which other evidence suggests was a short distance up river from the later Cavendish Bridge.[41] The crossing point would have varied as the river changed, but other references

27   10 & 11 William III, c. 20.
28   *VCH Staffs.*, IX, 27.
29   Melb. Hall Est. Office, X94/57/4/24.
30   *CJ*, 17, p. 586.
31   'Case in behalf of the bill for making a navigable cut from the Trent to the Mersey', printed in *The History of Inland Navigations* (1766), 71.
32   'Reasons humbly offer'd against the bill for the more speedy and effectually making navigable the river Trent' (*c.*1714) (Eighteenth-century Collections Online, accessed 11 Feb. 2016).
33   *VCH Staffs*, IX, 27.
34   'Case in behalf of the bill', 81–2.
35   *Reports of the late John Smeaton FRS made on various occasions in the course of his employment as a civil engineer*, I (London, 1812), 13–14.
36   *CJ*, 30, pp. 720–1.
37   *Derby Merc.*, 11 May 1770.
38   *St James's Chronicle or the British Evening Post,* 19 Jul. 1777.
39   *Report of the Royal Commission on Canals and Waterways* (Parl. Papers, Cd. 3184, XXXII, 1906), 231–2.
40   J. Farey, *General View on the Agriculture and Minerals of Derbyshire* (1811) I, 470.
41   *Cart. Chester* II, 475–7; ROLLR, DE 5251/2; P. Courtney, 'Crossing the Trent: the Hemington bridges in local and regional context', in Ripper and Cooper, 184.

in the same vicinity include 'Wiln Ford' in 1702,[42] and 'Dildrum ford' in 1717,[43] the latter apparently long-standing, as meadow called Dyndramford was recorded in 1441.[44]

The lord of Weston-on-Trent (Derb.) had a ferry valued at 13s. 4d. in 1086,[45] the figure suggesting it was on an important route, but its location cannot be pinpointed, as the bailiwick extended across the whole of the north bank of the river opposite Donington.[46] A ferry at 'Le Bargeford' in 1310 may have been a different service, as it was owned by the lord of Donington, who agreed to split the profits and costs with the lord of Weston to settle a dispute: two-thirds to Donington, and one-third to Weston. Although this ferry probably replaced a bridge in the north-east of the parish,[47] documentary evidence places it near the site of the later Cavendish Bridge, on the Leicester–Derby road.[48] It probably had a continuous existence from 1310 to 1760, as a ferry is recorded in 1331 and 1352,[49] the name Wilne ferry is documented regularly from 1377,[50] and can be firmly located near the Cavendish Bridge site by 1664. The ferry crossed the river by means of a large rope fixed to two posts.[51] When Alice Fosbrooke of 'Wilne Ferry House' died that year she owned 'the ferry boate', 'two parts' of each of two 'great' boats, suggesting the arrangement with the manor on the north bank continued, half of another great boat, two fishing boats, the ferry rope, tackle and two fishing nets, valued at £77 10s. She also had a wagon and six horses to carry goods.[52] The crossing later became known as Wilden Ferry.

The Wilne ferry crossing was fortified and garrisoned for the crown by Henry Hastings in 1643, who stationed 300 men here.[53] It was taken by parliament in 1644 after a siege of three days in which it was claimed that eight or nine men were killed, the governor and 180 other men taken prisoner, and the 'fort' slighted.[54] The following year, parliamentary forces under Sir John Gell prevented the Duke of Richmond and his brigade from crossing the Trent here on their way to Newark.[55] The crossing appears on Ogilby's road maps,[56] and became part of the Leicester–Derby turnpike in 1738. It fell out of service when Cavendish Bridge opened in 1760.

---

42 Derb. RO, D369/G/Maps/13.
43 Melb. Hall Est. Office, X94/57/4/33.
44 TNA, DL 29/184/2918, m. 1.
45 *Domesday*, 743.
46 *VCH Ches.*, III, 133, 144.
47 Ripper and Cooper, 223.
48 *Cart. Chester* II, 475–7; Ripper and Cooper, xv, 83.
49 *Cal. Inq. p.m.*, VII, 227; X, 45.
50 TNA, DL 29/183/2901, m. 1 (1377), TNA, DL 29/728/11987 (1400), DL 29/184/2923 (1450) and DL 28/26/1 (annually 1515–33).
51 'Reasons humbly offered'.
52 ROLLR, PR/I/62/62.
53 'A true relation of what service hath been done by Colonell Sir John Gell …', published in S. Glover, *History of the County of Derby* (Derby, 1829), 67.
54 J. Vicar, *God's Arke overtopping the World's Waves* (1645), 287 –8.
55 *Perfect Passages of Each Dayes Proceedings in Parliament*, 5 Nov. 1645.
56 J. Ogilby, *Britannia* (1698), 20 and plate 40.

Fords and Ferries at the Mills

Three and a half miles upriver, the Trent at King's Mills was affected by the mills, 'floodgates' and weirs, but there may have been a ford at low water after a flood of 1582 which 'turned the course of the Ryver of Trent another waye', and possibly earlier.[57] A garrison was also stationed here and the mills fortified for the crown in 1643, to intercept shipments of arms and prevent parliamentary troops crossing. The mills were captured by Sir John Gell in 1644, who claimed that 200 prisoners and arms were taken.[58] A ford near the mills was noted in 1904, although not in 1882 or 1923.[59]

A chain ferry at King's Mills was provided by the Hastings family in *c.*1790 for the convenience of the park estate. It was operated and maintained at the expense of the estate, although members of the public could use it for a small fee.[60] It moved a short distance further down-river between 1882 and 1904,[61] and ceased to operate in *c.*1942.[62]

Bridges

A succession of three bridges (the 'Hemington' bridges) was built immediately north-east of the settlement between the 11th and 13th centuries, the second and third of which were replacements following movement of the river. Each bridge served travellers between Leicester and Derby, and between Tamworth and Nottingham, perhaps replacing the ferry recorded in 1086. The first bridge, built in the late 11th or early 12th century, was just east of the 2015 parish boundary;[63] the second, standing from the late 12th to mid 13th century, was on that parish boundary,[64] while the third, immediately to its west, built in the mid 13th century on a slightly different orientation, was within Castle Donington.[65] The latter may be the bridge recorded in a charter of 1304,[66] which almost marks its passing, as archaeological evidence shows it suddenly collapsed, possibly during a severe flood recorded locally in 1309–10.[67] The replacements show the crossing was clearly important, but the final bridge may have been replaced for Derby travellers by the Wilne ferry at Donington from 1310, and Sawley ferry for Nottingham travellers from 1321,[68] which could adapt to the ever-changing river course in this area.

Parliament authorised a bridge at the Wilden ferry crossing in 1758.[69] William Cavendish, 4th duke of Devonshire, agreed to lend the full cost, estimated at £3,000, and

57   TNA, DL 44/355.
58   'A true relation', , App. 14, p. 66.
59   OS Map 6", Leics. IX.NE (1885 edn); (1904 edn); Derb. LVIII.NE (1924 edn).
60   *Derby Daily Telegraph*, 15 Jan. 1910, 19 Nov. 1929.
61   OS Map 6", Leics. IX.NE (1885 edn); (1904 edn).
62   F.B. Taylor, *Dwelling in the Past: Life in Castle Donington during the 1910 to 1930 period* (Castle Donington, 1995), 27.
63   Leics. and Rutl. HER, MLE 9629; S. Ripper and R. Darrah, 'Bridge I: the late 11th- to early 12th-century bridge', in Ripper and Cooper, 13.
64   Leics. and Rutl. HER, MLE 9685.
65   Ibid., MLE 9684.
66   TNA, DL 25/1773.
67   Ripper and Cooper, xv, 83.
68   TNA, SC 6/1132/5.
69   31 Geo. II c. 59.

Figure 2 *Cavendish Bridge in 1947.*

Map 2 *Cavendish Bridge in 1884.*

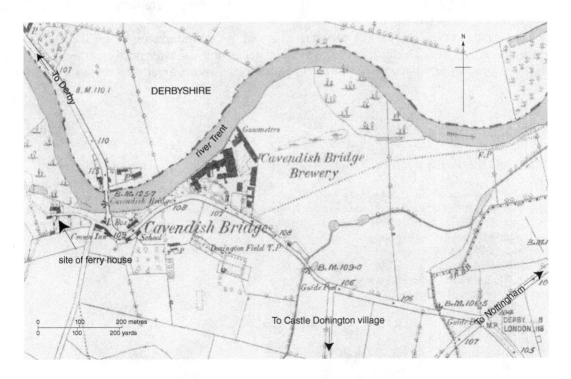

it became known as Cavendish Bridge, after its patron. Although some watermen tried to obstruct its construction,[70] the bridge opened in 1760.[71] It collapsed in the floods of 1947 (Fig. 2),[72] when the Royal Engineers provided a temporary bailey bridge.[73] As the original approach on the Donington side was not suited to the faster speed of motor vehicles (Map 2),[74] the opportunity was taken to replace it with a new bridge to the east, which opened in 1957.[75]

Roads before 1900

The road from Leicester to Derby formed part of the route from London to Carlisle, and crossed the northern tip of the parish to reach Wilden Ferry.[76] The section between Loughborough and the ferry became Leicestershire's second turnpike in 1738,[77] and a toll house was erected on the Donington side of the crossing.[78] The tolls remained unchanged when Cavendish Bridge replaced the ferry in 1760.[79] The Turnpike Act governing this section of the road between Loughborough and Cavendish Bridge was repealed in 1885, under legislation of 1884.[80]

The alignment of the presumed original nucleated settlement along High Street and Bondgate suggests this was also an important route at an early date. The road connected Tamworth, Ashby-de-la-Zouch and villages in the south-west to the 'Hemington' bridges and later to the ford near Sawley for travellers to Nottingham or, by branching off, to Wilden ferry for Derby. The road to Nottingham was turnpiked in 1760,[81] and three 19th-century cast iron mileposts giving the distances to Tamworth and to Nottingham survive at one-mile intervals across the parish.[82] Only one Donington resident, yeoman John Matchett, was a subscriber to the Trust.[83] Sawley ferry was replaced by Harrington Bridge in 1791.[84] The Tamworth to Nottingham turnpike was disestablished in 1880, by an Act of Parliament of 1878.[85]

The east–west road across the parish to King's Mills continued west of the Trent, and provided access from Derbyshire pastures and Chellaston's alabaster mines to the fulling and gypsum mills. It may also have been a long-distance route, extending eastwards (as

---

70　*Derby Merc.*, 31 Aug. 1759.
71　Derb. RO, D533/A/TT/16, pp. 3–4, 7, 25.
72　*Derby Daily Telegraph*, 22 Mar. 1947.
73　Ibid., 7 Apr. 1947.
74　OS Map 6", Leics. V.SW (1884 edn).
75　Film of opening: http://www.macearchive.org/Archive/Title/midlands-news-27081957-opening-of-cavendish-bridge-shardlow/MediaEntry/2121.html (accessed 19 Jul. 2014).
76　Ogilby, *Britannia*, 20, plate 40.
77　11 Geo. II c. 33.
78　ROLLR, DG9 Ma/L/1.
79　Toll house plaque, preserved at new bridge.
80　47 & 48 Vict. c. 52, sch. 2.
81　33 Geo. II c. 41.
82　Leics. and Rutl. HER, MLE 11304; MLE 11142; MLE 11292.
83　ROLLR, 6D 45/3.
84　28 Geo. III, c. 80; Derb. RO, D533/A/TT/17.
85　41 & 42 Vict. c. 62, sch. 5.

a footpath in 2015, blocked by the M1 motorway) to Kegworth and beyond, for either Melton Mowbray or the Vale of Belvoir.

The possession of copyhold land in Donington gave grazing rights in Derby Hills, but no early transhumance routes can be identified from maps, other than a footpath through the park, which terminates at King's Newton.

Roads since 1900

The minor road from Donington to Diseworth closed following the creation of East Midlands Airport in 1965.[86] The M1 motorway from Watford to Kegworth also opened in 1965. It passes outside the parish, with a junction (J24) two miles east of Castle Donington. The motorway was extended to Nottingham in 1966, and Leeds in 1968.[87] A new junction on the M1 two miles south-east of Donington (J23A) opened in 1991,[88] providing access to a trunk road (A42) linking the M1 to the M42 (for Birmingham and the south-west), also serving the village and airport. Plans made in the early 1970s for a motorway between the M1 at Kegworth and the M6 near Stoke on Trent were cancelled in 1976,[89] but later resurrected in a downgraded and revised form. The eastern part of this road (A50 Derby by-pass) opened in 1997,[90] running south of Cavendish Bridge on an elevated road across the north of the parish, with a further motorway junction (J24A) where it meets the M1, giving three M1 junctions within two miles of the village. Following these changes, the 1957 (Cavendish) bridge served local traffic only.

Road Transport Services

By the 1820s, coaches on the turnpike road from Nottingham to Birmingham stopped at the Moira Arms at 10 am daily except Sundays, while coaches travelling in the opposite direction stopped at 3 pm, providing some boost to trade but not the more lucrative meal times or overnight stops. The London to Derby coaches travelled along the turnpike road crossing the north of the parish, stopping in Kegworth.[91] With the coming of the railway, coach services reduced to three times each week by 1841 and ceased by 1848.[92]

'Walkers' ran three times a week on the Leicester–Derby road across Cavendish Bridge in 1794, although it is not clear whether this was a coach or carrier service.[93] Carriers ran between Donington and Nottingham, Loughborough and Derby in the 1820s,[94] and Ashby-de-la-Zouch was added to the list of destinations by 1855.[95] Carrier services declined sharply after the railway station opened in 1869, and the only service

---

86   OS Map 1:25 000, SK 42 (1968 edn); (1972 edn).
87   http://www.cbrd.co.uk/motorway/m1/timeline (accessed 24 Jul. 2014).
88   Ex inf. Highways Agency, 2015.
89   Leics. CC, *Leicestershire Structure Plan* (1974), 8; http://www.cbrd.co.uk/motorway/a50 (accessed 7 Dec. 2015).
90   http://www.cbrd.co.uk/motorway/a50 (accessed 7 Dec. 2015).
91   Pigot & Co., *Dir. Leics. and Rutl.* (1828–9), 477.
92   Ibid. (1841), 9; (1848), 2520–1.
93   *Universal Brit. Dir.* (1794), 591.
94   Pigot & Co., *Dir. Leics. and Rutl.* (1828–9), 477.
95   *PO Dir. Leics. and Rutl.* (1855), 26.

operating in 1876 was daily to Derby.[96] A twice-weekly service to Nottingham was added by 1916,[97] but by 1936 the only service ran from the station.[98] No service ever appears to have been provided to Leicester.

Early bus services were linked to the railway network. The Midland Railway operated a horse-drawn omnibus from Donington to Kegworth station by 1846.[99] By the 1860s there was a daily omnibus to Derby station, a weekly service to Loughborough and a twice-weekly service to Nottingham.[100] A service linking local villages was in place by 1928, with daily bus services from Castle Donington to Long Eaton (Derb.), Diseworth, Hathern and Long Whatton,[101] with Loughborough added after the closure of Donington's railway station in 1930.[102] Public transport to the airport was poor in 1976,[103] but formed the focus of local bus services in 2015: 'Skylink' services operated by the 'trentbarton' bus company linked the airport and Castle Donington to Nottingham, Long Eaton, Derby, Loughborough, Leicester and local villages,[104] but no bus service connected the village to East Midlands Parkway railway station. A taxi shuttle service between the airport and East Midlands Parkway station commenced in 2015.[105]

Railways

The Midland Railway opened a station at Kegworth in 1840, 4 miles from Castle Donington, for trains to Leicester, Derby or Nottingham.[106] Following the collapse of the 'warp blonde' lace industry in the 1850s, many people moved from Donington to find work elsewhere,[107] and remaining residents petitioned the Midland Railway in 1862 in the hope that a railway line and village station would arrest the trend.[108] The company began buying land in the north of the parish in 1868 for a line linking Derby with Trent station, south of Long Eaton, for trains to Loughborough and Nottingham.[109] This opened, with a station at Castle Donington, in 1869. The station's name was changed to Castle Donington and Shardlow in 1898,[110] but this failed to increase business. The station closed to passengers in 1930,[111] other than occasional services for events at Donington Park, but the line remained open.[112] These occasional passenger services

96   *PO Dir. Leics. and Rutl.* (1876), 344.
97   *Kelly's Dir. Leics. and Rutl.* (1916), 55.
98   Ibid. (1936), 56.
99   W. White, *Dir. Leics. and Rutl.* (Sheffield, 1846), 342.
100 Ibid. (1863), 487.
101 *Kelly's Dir. Leics. and Rutl.* (1928), 58.
102 Ibid. (1932), 58; (1941), 55.
103 Leics. CC, *Leicestershire Structure Plan* (1974), 29.
104 https://www.trentbarton.co.uk/services/skylinknottingham/timetable; https://www.trentbarton.co.uk/services/skylinkderby/timetable (accessed 5 Nov. 2015).
105 https://www.eastmidlandstrains.co.uk/information/media/news/Launch-of-New-Parkway-Railink---Connect-East-Midlands-Parkway-and-East-Midlands-Airport/ (accessed 31 Dec. 2015).
106 R.V.J. Butt, *The Directory of Railway Stations* (Sparkford, 1995), 129.
107 Below, 59.
108 For example, *Derby Daily Telegraph*, 11 Oct. 1862.
109 Melb. Hall Est. Office, X94/42/1, pp. 454–9.
110 A. Moore, *Leicestershire Stations: An Historical Perspective* (Narborough, 1998), 91.
111 Butt, *The Directory*, 55.
112 For example, *Derby Daily Telegraph*, 7 Jul. 1934.

ceased in 1960, and the platform was removed.[113] In 2015 the nearest stations were East Midlands Parkway (6 miles) and Long Eaton (also 6 miles), both serving Leicester, London, Nottingham, Derby and Sheffield. In 1868, the Midland Railway also opened a station in Melbourne for trains to Derby, with the line extended through the edge of the parish to Ashby-de-la-Zouch in 1874.[114] This also closed to passengers in 1930.[115]

Following the construction of Castle Donington power station adjacent to the line, trains transported several thousand tons of coal to the site each week between 1958 and 1994,[116] and carried away ash.[117] The Central Electricity Generating Board built their own sidings and internal lines to deliver the coal to the generating units,[118] and used a pair of steam locomotives until at least 1988, making these among the last used in British industry.[119] The railway remained in use in 2015, and Marks & Spencer, who opened a distribution centre in 2012 on the former power station site, had their own rail freight terminal.

Airport

The Air Ministry purchased 440 a. across Castle Donington, Lockington cum Hemington and Kegworth parishes in 1942, opening an airfield in 1943 as a satellite to the RAF's Operational Training Unit at Wymeswold.[120] Derby Borough Council entered negotiations in 1961 to purchase the airfield, to replace a civil airfield at Burnaston. Ambitious plans to create a freight and passenger terminal to serve Leicester, Nottingham and Derby were agreed in 1963 by the city councils of Derby and Nottingham and the county councils of Derbyshire, Leicestershire and Nottinghamshire, with costs shared.[121] East Midlands Airport opened in 1965.[122] A runway extension was approved by the Board of Trade in 1970,[123] and two large package tour operators, Thomson and Horizon Holidays, began to offer holidays flying from the airport in 1970 and 1971.[124] A cargo terminal opened in 1973.[125]

In 1993, seeking greater investment than the councils could provide, the airport was sold to the National Express Group, for a reported £27 million.[126] Over the next five years, National Express invested £4 million in the site,[127] developing a 54 a. business

---

113 Moore, *Leicestershire Stations*, 92.
114 Ibid., 87.
115 Butt, *The Directory*, 157.
116 Below, 67.
117 *The Times*, 15 Dec. 1969.
118 OS Map, 1:10,000, SK 42 NW (1989 edn).
119 BBC Television, Lines of Industry (1988), clip at https://www.youtube.com/watch?v=hzG4JBPBNI4 (accessed 12 Dec. 2015).
120 K. Delve, *The Military Airfields of Britain: East Midlands* (Marlborough, 2008), 87.
121 TNA, MAF 140/42.
122 *The Times*, 27 Mar. 1965.
123 R. Walker, *The Airport: Serving the East Midlands for 40 years* (Castle Donington, 2005), 49.
124 *The Times*, 16 Sept. 1970; 1 May 1972.
125 Walker, *The Airport*, 50.
126 *The Times*, 22 Jul. 1993.
127 *The Times*, 14 Oct. 1998.

park with Wilson Bowden on adjacent land,[128] and creating a parcel handling facility as a joint venture with the international parcel company, DHL.[129] In 2001, when National Express sold the airport to Manchester Airports Group,[130] the airport was handling nearly 200,000 tonnes of freight and mail each year, and serving 2.38 million passengers, mostly on scheduled or package holiday flights.[131] Passenger numbers increased to over 4 million in the early 2000s through the low-cost airline boom, with EasyJet, bmibaby and Ryanair all offering flights from East Midlands by 2004.[132] In 2015, East Midlands Airport provided domestic services and flights to 26 different countries, through 30 different airlines and tour operators, including bmi regional, Flybe, Jet2 and Ryanair.[133] Aided by its position in the centre of the country and a good road network, it was also the second busiest cargo airport in the UK,[134] handling 300,000 tonnes annually.[135]

Post and Telecommunications

The mail-coach crossed the Trent at Wilden ferry (later Cavendish Bridge), where there was a private receiving house. Letters in the 'Loughborough bag' from London were left there in 1701 for the Cokes at Melbourne Hall,[136] and for Donington Park and the village. Trains to Derby replaced the mail-coach from 1840, but Derby's postmaster arranged a private conveyance to provide a service to the Park and village. The receiving house disappears from records in 1843, when John Hunt was appointed as receiver in Castle Donington; he had been the post office keeper there since at least 1823.[137] The post office was in Bondgate,[138] moving to Borough Street in 1877 when Mrs Hunt resigned the office.[139] It remained in Borough Street in 2015.[140]

The Royal Mail began to use East Midlands Airport in 1980, distributing post to UK airports by overnight flights. A 10-year agreement was signed in 1987 and a mail sorting office built.[141] Subsequent road improvements enabled this to become a major distribution hub, which in 2015 received 67 tonnes of first class post by road and 50 tonnes by air each night on 11 aircraft.[142]

A system of 'telephonic communication' between the water pumping station at Stanton-by-Bridge and the reservoir at Castle Donington was agreed by the District

---

128 Walker, *The Airport*, 143.
129 *The Times*, 14 Oct. 1998.
130 *Manchester Airports Group, Annual Rpt and Accts 2000–01*, 6.
131 Walker, *The Airport*, 145, 167.
132 *Manchester Airports Group, Annual Rpt and Accts 2003–04*, 4.
133 http://www.eastmidlandsairport.com/ (accessed 9 Nov. 2015).
134 *Manchester Airports Group, Annual Rpt and Accts 2012–13*, 7.
135 http://www.eastmidlandsairport.com/emaweb.nsf/Content/FactsAndFigures (accessed 5 Nov. 2015).
136 *HMC, Cowper*, II, 430–2, 434–6, 438–41, 443.
137 J. Soer, *The Royal Mail in Leicestershire and Rutland* (1997), 68–9.
138 W. White, *Dir. Leics. and Rutl.* (Sheffield, 1846), 340.
139 *Leic. Chron.*, 14 Apr. 1877.
140 http://www.openinghourspostoffice.co.uk/Post+Office+Castle+Donington+-+Derby+(Derbyshire)/ DE74%202LB/Derby/11444 (accessed 3 Oct.2015).
141 R. Walker, *The Airport: Serving the East Midlands for 40 years* (Castle Donington, 2005), 65, 105.
142 http://www.eastmidlandsairport.com/emacargo.nsf/content/customer_royalmail (accessed 8 Dec. 2015.

Council in 1900.[143] A telephone 'call office' opened in Castle Donington post office in 1908, with trunk connections through Derby.[144] A telephone exchange later opened on Park Lane, and became a satellite of Derby in 1970, taking Derby telephone numbers.[145] It moved from Park Lane to Delven Lane in *c.*1972.[146] Broadband internet services were available from 2001,[147] fibre optic broadband was available in parts of the village from 2013,[148] and 'superfast' broadband was rolled out from 2014.[149]

Settlement

In terms of the built environment, the modern parish falls into five 'zones': the park in the west (including the motor-racing circuit and the small settlement at King's Mills), the airport in the south-east, the low-lying northern ground (including the settlement at Cavendish Bridge), the expanding village in the centre, and the commercial zone to the north and north-west of the village, the latter mostly within two business 'parks' west of Station Road, straddling the railway line.

Early Settlement

Early settlements are often a feature of river valleys, and Castle Donington is the westernmost of three adjacent villages along the Trent valley with the early ending -ingtūn (the others being Hemington and Lockington), its prefix being the personal name Dunn. To the south, the 'Walton' in the name Isley Walton means 'a farmstead of Britons', suggesting a degree of cultural contrasts in the early Middle Ages.[150]

Extensive residential and commercial development since the early 1970s has presented many opportunities for archaeologists ahead of building, and substantial evidence of early settlement has been found (Map 3). To the north of the railway line there were a series of settlements from the late Neolithic to the early Anglo-Saxon period. Finds include an early Bronze Age burial site with cremation urn,[151] two late Bronze Age or early Iron Age round houses with a large quantity of pottery,[152] and a series of pits and post-holes with pits containing over 3 kg of late Bronze Age pottery sherds.[153] Later settlement is suggested by pits containing Iron Age pottery,[154] a late Iron Age or early

---

143 *Leic. Chron.*, 4 Aug. 1900.
144 BT Archives, PO Circulars, 1908.
145 *PO Gaz.*, 21 Jan. 1970.
146 OS Map, 1:2500, SK 4427 SW SE (1961 edn), (1971 edn), (1980 edn).
147 http://broadband4u.net/Castle-Donington-Telephone-Exchange-EMCASTL.html (accessed 3 Oct. 2015).
148 http://www.techworld.com/news/networking/bt-upgrade-another-99-exchanges-for-fibre-broadband-3425688/ (accessed 11 Aug. 2015).
149 http://www.ispreview.co.uk/index.php/2014/10/leicestershire-uk-confirm-next-phase-2-areas-fibre-broadband-rollout.html (accessed 11 Aug. 2015).
150 B. Cox, *A Dictionary of Leicestershire and Rutland Place-names* (Nottingham, 2005), 22, 48, 64, 53.
151 Leics. and Rutl. HER, MLE 9676.
152 Ibid., MLE 9675, 9681.
153 Ibid., MLE 9677.
154 Ibid., MLE 9680.

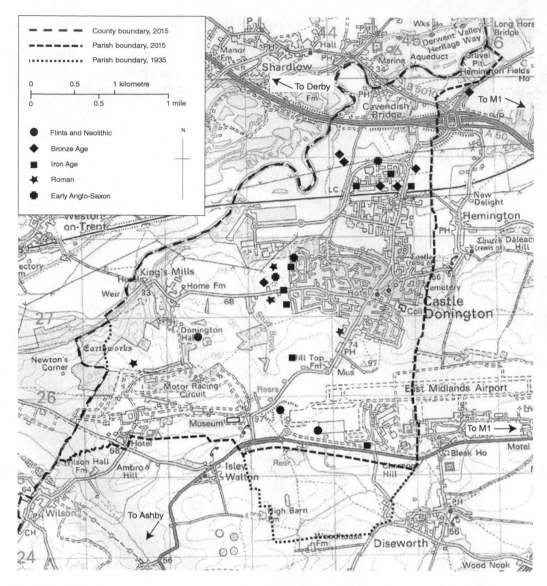

Map 3 *Castle Donington in 2015, superimposed with archaeological discoveries to the 7th century (archaeological sites not to scale)* (© *Crown copyright 2016, OS licence 100057794*).

Roman quern,[155] and two early Anglo-Saxon buildings containing early Anglo-Saxon pottery and loom weights.[156] Slightly further north, two Bronze Age burnt mounds have also been found.[157]

Immediately to the north of Park Lane, pits and sherds of late Neolithic or early Bronze Age pottery including a rare coil-built beaker have been found,[158] and a quantity of Iron Age and a little Roman pottery.[159] Slightly further north, an Iron Age and early Roman settlement site has been found,[160] near Anglo-Saxon pottery and slag from early metal-working.[161] To the south of the lane, Iron Age pottery and a Roman boundary ditch have been discovered,[162] and an area in Donington Park, just to the north of the motor-racing circuit, has yielded substantial deposits of Roman building materials, with pottery indicative of continuous occupation throughout the Roman period.[163]

Excavation at the airport revealed evidence for two phases of Iron Age field systems, and the two areas together yielded 500 sherds of mid to late Iron Age pottery and 200 sherds of early Roman pottery.[164] Post holes, pits and sherds from the late Neolithic or early Bronze Age have been discovered a short distance to the west.[165] Further evidence of early settlement may be obscured by the village. The paucity of later finds in outlying parts of the parish is consistent with, but not necessarily evidence for, the formation of a nucleated village on the present site (where there has been little archaeological investigation) shortly after the 7th century.

The Medieval Town

Donington had the potential to become a successful town: it was near several river crossings, under the protection of the castle and its major landowners, and 8 miles from the nearest market, at Derby (across the Trent).[166] Topography and street names suggest the original village stretched along Bondgate, which also carried the town brook. The castle was probably built in the 1140s, and a hospital 500 yd. to its west is believed to have been founded by 1190, suggesting early urban ambitions. Borough Street was probably laid out immediately south of the castle in the late 12th or 13th century as a trading area, and a charter for a market and fair was granted in 1278.[167] Unlike the steep-sided Bondgate, Borough Street forms a wide plateau for traders. Its name, width, long thin plots abutting its western side and rentals identifying burgage tenure, all characteristic

---

155 Ibid., MLE 6548.
156 Ibid., MLE 9678.
157 Ibid., MLE 9682, 9683.
158 Ibid., MLE 10293.
159 Ibid., MLE 10295.
160 Ibid., MLE 16904.
161 Ibid., MLE 10297; 10296.
162 Ibid., MLE 20672, 20673, 20674.
163 Ibid., MLE 4432.
164 Ibid., MLE 5931.
165 Ibid., MLE 9672.
166 S. Letters, *Gazetteer of Markets & Fairs in England and Wales to 1516*, http://www.history.ac.uk/cmh/ gaz/gazweb2.html (accessed 7 May 2014).
167 *Cal. Chart.* 1257–1300, 207.

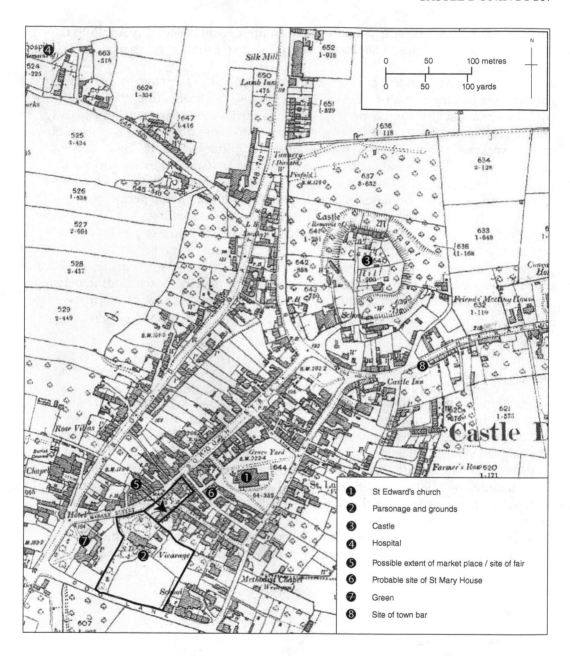

1 St Edward's church
2 Parsonage and grounds
3 Castle
4 Hospital
5 Possible extent of market place / site of fair
6 Probable site of St Mary House
7 Green
8 Site of town bar

Map 4 *Key locations in the medieval town.*

of urban settlement, suggest that this was intended to be the heart of a planned town,[168] and its continuous frontages, evident in 1779,[169] and probably standing on much earlier footings, suggest the town was successful in its early years. The slight curve apparent on some of the western plot boundaries is unlikely to indicate former arable land, as the ground is too steep.

Borough Street narrows at both ends, perhaps as a result of early encroachment. The market place is shown on the inclosure map of 1779,[170] confirming that it pre-dated the re-establishment of the market in 1814, and may once have been much larger (Map 4).[171] A town bar or gate was south-east of the castle, and probably erected before 1301, when the name Richard at the Gate appears.[172] Population growth and difficulty in controlling tenure resulted in development on former arable land to the south-east of the castle, beyond the town bar, and by 1322, there were at least 36 cottages 'outside the gate of the vill on le Barrewonge' (later Barroon), with one of those cottages divided into eight parts.[173]

The parsonage stood in large grounds just off the market place, with the green to its west, recorded in 1490.[174] Clapgun Street was probably a back lane to the fields, although at least one property in this street was held by burgage tenure.[175] Map 4 also shows the probable location of St Mary's House, which may have been used for meetings of a town guild from the early 14th century.

Town and Village from *c.*1500

Castle Donington possesses 77 listed domestic buildings, and over 200 other buildings identified as having architectural or historic interest.[176] Only a flavour of their variety and quality can be given here. The numbers in bold parentheses below relate to their position on Map 5, which covers just the village core. The narrow streets in the centre of the village are typical of former medieval towns, but the overwhelming impression from the architecture is that this was a prosperous Georgian settlement. Behind those facades, the earliest domestic properties are timber-framed, and include several of cruck construction, which have survived because tougher economic conditions from the 1830s favoured repair over replacement. 'Yorkshire' sash windows, which slide sideways to open, remained a feature in several older properties in 2015.

Domestic Buildings

A small number of medieval buildings survive, at least in part. A cruck frame in the external wall of a house at 52 Spittal (Fig. 4).may be part of the medieval hospital

168 TNA, DL 43/6/4.
169 ROLLR, DE 5251/2.
170 ROLLR, DE 5251/2.
171 OS Map 25", Leics. X.1 (1921 edn).
172 TNA, DL 25/1771.
173 TNA, SC 6/1146/9, m. 3.
174 TNA, DL 30/80/1091, m. 2.
175 TNA, DL 44/192 (unpag., Thomas Paynter).
176 Ryder (1997); Ryder (2000).

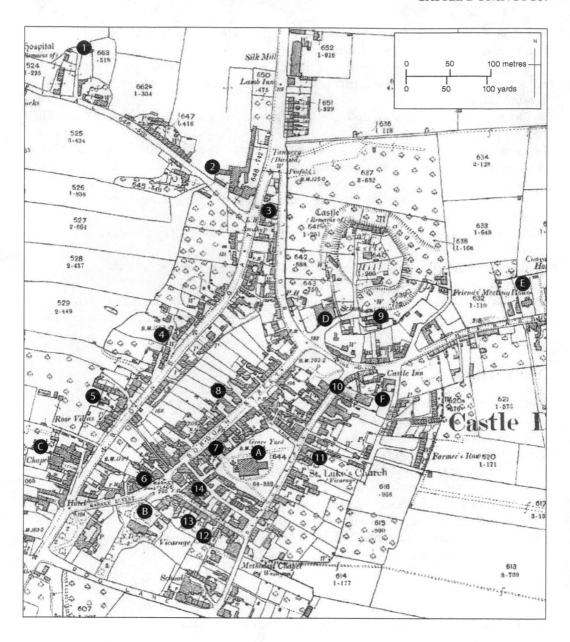

Map 5 *Central Castle Donington. Numbers relate to buildings described in this chapter. Letters mark places of worship described in the Religious History chapter.*

Figure 3 *Pool Close Farmhouse (88 High Street) dates from the early 15th century.*

buildings **(1)**.[177] Pool Close Farmhouse (Fig. 3), at the southern end of the old inclosures along High Street, has been described as 'arguably the most significant historic building in the village, after the parish church'.[178] It appears to have had an open hall at the centre of its three-bay range, with a two-bay cross wing to the north. Timbers have been dated by dendrochronology to the early 15th century. As a farmhouse, its owners had no need to be in the more crowded urban area. The house was clad in brick in the 17th and 18th centuries.[179] Within the village centre, 7–9 The Moat **(9)** may date from the late 15th or 16th century.[180] A late medieval hall and cross-wing house survives within 37–39 Clapgun Street **(11)**, with a later shop front inserted.[181]

From the 16th century, 1 Apiary Gate **(14)** has a ridge piece in the one surviving cruck bay which was felled *c*.1512–35. This may have been a three-bay house set at right angles to the road; a wooden mullion survives at the rear.[182] A two-bay cruck house, 29–31 Bondgate **(5),** contains timbers felled in the winter of 1553–4. It was extended to the north in the late 17th century and to the south in the 18th century; its cellars are cut

177   Ryder (1997), 66; NHL no. 1361339, 52, Spittal, accessed 2 Mar. 2016.
178   Ryder (2000), 5.
179   Ryder (2000), 23-4; Pevsner, 125; NHL, no. 1101785, Pool Close Farmhouse: 2 Mar. 2016.
180   Ryder (1997), 62-3; NHL, no. 1101778, 7 and 9, Moat: 2 Mar. 2016.
181   Ryder (1997), 45-6; NHL, no. 1361369, 37 and 39, Clapgun Street: 2 Mar. 2016.
182   N. Alcock and D. Miles, *The Medieval Peasant House in Midland England* (Oxford, 2013), individual house report CAS-A; M. Pollard, Derb. Buildings Record 24 (1981); Ryder, 18; NHL, no. 1074132, 1, Apiary Gate: 2 Mar. 2016.

Figure 4 *Timber frames: from the left, 52 Spittal, 20 High Street (Key House).*

Figure 5 *Dalbie House, 72 High Street, built in 1735.*

from the rock.[183] On High Street, the core of Key House (Fig. 4) is late 16th-century and stands on a stone base; the porch, bearing the date 1595, is from a former farmhouse on the opposite side of the road.[184] Charnwood Cottage, also on High Street, is timber-framed and thatched, originally of two bays, and is probably 16th-century.[185]

Probate inventories reveal that the typical house of the 17th-century yeoman or husbandman had three bays, with a hall, parlour, kitchen, and chambers over. The 1660s to 1680s saw several properties extended, with Alice Fosbrooke (d. 1664), John Dalbey (d. 1667), Thomas Bucknall (d. 1673) and Samuel Matchett (d. 1687) having parlours and chambers described as 'new' when they died.[186] Surviving houses from this period which are timber-framed or incorporate part of a timber frame include 6–8 Apiary Gate (**12**), of 16th or 17th-century post and truss construction,[187] 59–61 Bondgate (**4**), where the south bay was extended to create a shop in the early 19th century,[188] and 4–6 Spittal (**2**), a semi-detached pair with square timber-framed panels, probably built in the mid or late 17th century, which may 'mark the transition between timber-frame and brick building at vernacular level'.[189]

Walls, footings and plinths built from the local sandstone are common, but there are few stone-built houses. Two exceptions are 13 Clapgun Street (**10**), rebuilt in stone in the 17th century on an earlier cross-passage plan, reusing a cruck blade as a roof truss,[190] and 4 Apiary Gate (**13**) with adjacent barn, built of squared sandstone in the late 17th-century.[191]

The 18th century was a period of prosperity, and is well represented. There are several fine examples of large 18th-century houses in red brick, built for factory owners, prosperous farmers and a growing professional class. On High Street, number 72 (Dalbie House, Fig. 5) is of three storeys, built in 1735 with interior wall paintings including a village scene with a castle, perhaps representing Castle Donington,[192] and number 73 (Peppercorn House) is also three storeys, built in c.1770.[193] In the centre of the village, and similar in style and period, are 15 Market Street (**6**), of three storeys in a paler brick, the central bay with pediment,[194] 41 Borough Street (**8**), with later shop-front inserted,[195]

183 Alcock and Miles, *The Medieval Peasant*, CAS-B; B. Hutton, Derb. Buildings Rec. 23 (1982); Ryder (1997), 29; NHL, no. 1100258, Cruck House: 2 Mar. 2016.

184 J. Heath and B. Hutton, Derb. Buildings Rec. 49 (1989); Ryder (2000), 15–16; Pevsner, 125; NHL, no. 1101468, The Key House: 2 Mar. 2016.

185 Ryder (2000), 14; Pevsner, 125; NHL, no. 1361335 Charnwood Cottage: 2 Mar. 2016.

186 ROLLR, PR/I/62/62, PR/I/69/34, P/I/74/131, PR/I/90/41.

187 Ryder (1997), 21–22; NHL, no. 1074133, 6 and 8 Apiary Gate: 2 Mar. 2016.

188 Ryder (1997), 31; NHL, no. 1074125 Nos 59 and 61 Bondgate: 2 Mar. 2016.

189 Ryder (1997), 64–5, 16; NHL, no. 1074161, 4 and 6 Spittal: 2 Mar.2016.

190 Ryder (1997), 43–4.

191 Ryder (1997), 19–20; NHL, no. 1100312, Number 4, with storehouse adjoining, 4, Apiary Gate: 2 Mar. 2016.

192 Ryder (2000), 21, 13–14; NHL, no. 1074152, Number 72, and attached outbuildings, High Street: 2 Mar. 2016.

193 NHL, no. 1074148, 71, High Street (sic): 2 Mar. 2016.

194 Ryder (1997), 60; NHL, No. 1074156, 17 Market Street (sic): 2 Mar. 2016.

195 Ryder (1997), 36; Pevsner, 124; NHL, No. 1074137, 41 Borough Street: 2 Mar. 2016.

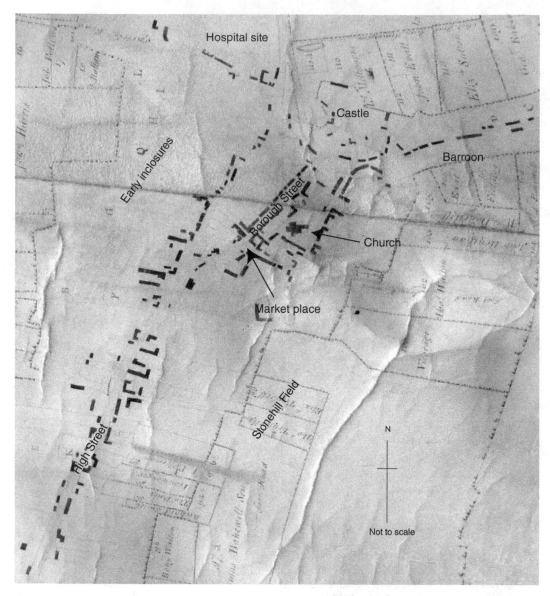

Map 6 *Part of the inclosure map, showing Castle Donington in 1779.*

and a terrace of Georgian shops, 18-26 Borough Street (7), an unusual survival but much altered.[196]

The inclosure map shows High Street was well developed by 1779 (Map 6). The lace boom of the early 19th century was accompanied by significant expansion of the village, from 416 houses in 1801 to 754 by 1841, which included houses built on the east side of Bondgate, following the culverting of the town brook between 1812 and 1814.[197] The most notable addition in this period was Crown House (3), built in 1818 with 'spectacular plaster decoration' inside two front rooms and an external plaster tympanum, by John Sutton, the master plasterer at Donington Hall.[198] The contraction in population from 1841, following the collapse of the lace trade, resulted in the demolition of over 130 homes between 1851 and 1861.[199] Although a few houses were built on Station Road and Mount Pleasant in the early 20th century,[200] there were still only 636 dwellings in the village in 1921.[201]

The 1920s and early 1930s saw private building of villa-type houses on Park Lane, and the construction of Donington's first council houses, in Barroon, Victoria Street, Eastway and Moira Dale, on the east of the village.[202] Further council houses and speculative private development anticipated the opening of the power station in 1958. By 1963, two large mixed housing estates had been built in the east and south-east of the village, with another off Park Lane.[203] The pace of house-building was deliberately slackened in the 1980s,[204] but the early 21st century has seen further expansion, with plans for a residential development of 895 houses off Park Lane approved in 2013.[205]

Industrial Development

Anticipating a decline in the Leicestershire coal industry, the county council sought to attract employers to north-west Leicestershire from the late 1960s,[206] partly through the development of a 'freight village' of offices and warehouses near the airport.[207] This became Pegasus Business Park, which covered 26 ha. in 2015, with a further 10 ha. available for airport-related development.[208] To the north of the village, 70 a. (28 ha.) west of the through road was earmarked for industrial development in the 1960s.[209] This became Trent Lane Industrial Estate (17.6 ha. south of the railway), built in the 1970s and early 1980s,[210] and Willow Farm Business Park (23.5 ha. north of the railway), comprising

196 Ryder (1997), 38.
197 Town bk.
198 Ryder (1997), 26; Pevsner, 125; NHL, no. 1074136, Crown House: 2 Mar. 2016.
199 Census.
200 OS Map, 1:2500, Leics. X.1 (1903 edn), (1921 edn).
201 Census co. reports.
202 *Derby Daily Telegraph*, 10 Dec. 1929; *Loughborough Echo*, 8 Sept. 1939.
203 OS Map, 1:10,000, SK 42 NW (1963 edn).
204 NW Leics. Northern Parishes Local Plan: Written Statement (1984), 38.
205 http://www.bbc.co.uk/news/uk-england-22870081 (accessed 28 Jan. 2016).
206 The Leicester and Leicestershire Sub-regional Planning Study (1969), 87–90.
207 *The Times*, 10 Sept.1968.
208 NW Leics. Local Plan, Draft (2015), 64; CDPC, Annual Rept, 2010–11.
209 Leics. CC Planning Dept, 'Castle Donington Village Plan' (1964), 6.
210 NW Leics. Northern Parishes Local Plan: Written Statement (1984), 15, 16, 20, 38

larger units, added from the late 1990s. A distribution depot for the retailer Marks and Spencer of 900,000 sq. ft opened on the former power station site in 2012.[211]

King's Mills and Cavendish Bridge

It is possible that the mill recorded in 1086 was in the north-east of the parish,[212] but there has almost certainly been a watermill at King's Mills since at least the mid 14th century. Three taxpayers bore the name del Milne or del Mylnes in 1377, as well as two men called Milner,[213] suggesting a secondary settlement, and manorial accounts record cottages at Milnethorpe from at least 1420.[214] A map of 1735 shows a terrace of cottages where a later 19th-century terrace stands (see also Map 10).[215]

John Campion lived at Wilden Ferry in 1565,[216] 1.6 miles north of the centre of Castle Donington village, and Leonard Fosbrooke erected outbuildings, perhaps warehouses, there in 1662.[217] In 1664, there was a substantial house, with three of its 12 rooms described as 'new'.[218] This was rebuilt in the late 18th century in red brick, the windows flanking the central door creating a venetian-style surround.[219] The only other buildings in this part of the parish in 1779 were the toll house on the approach to Cavendish Bridge, with two adjacent buildings.[220] A three-storey warehouse was built alongside the Trent in the late 18th century, and converted to flats in the 1970s.[221] The settlement grew after the opening of the brewery in 1815,[222] and by 1841 it contained 22 households.[223] There was also an auxiliary hospital here during the First World War.[224]

Population

Donington was a large village in 1086, when 30 villans, 11 bordars, 5 sokemen and a priest were recorded, suggesting a population of around 200 people.[225] The addition of two aisles to the parish church in the 13th century may indicate population growth as well as liturgical change. There were 280 people assessed for the poll tax in 1377, making

---

211 http://www.leicestermercury.co.uk/pound-82-5m-deal-sell-ex-M-amp-S-warehouse-Castle/story-20335494-detail/story.html; http://allportcargoservices.com/retailnews/allport-knowledge/archives/mon/5/yr/2013/1 (accessed 1 Jul. 2014).
212 Cooper and Ripper, 39.
213 *Poll Taxes 1377–81* (ed.) Fenwick, I, 484–91.
214 TNA, DL 29/183/2903.
215 ROLLR, DG 30/Ma/64/2; NHL, no. 1347805, The Cottages at King's Mills: 2 Mar. 2016.
216 ROLLR, 5D 33/210/f/6/1.
217 Town bk; 'Reasons humbly offer'd'.
218 ROLLR, PR/I/62/62.
219 NHL, No. 1074139, Three Cranes: 2 Mar. 2016.
220 ROLLR, DE 5152/2.
221 North West Leicestershire District Council, *Cavendish Bridge Conservation Area Appraisal and Study* (2001), 5.
222 Pigot & Co., *Dir. Leics. and Rutl.* (1835), 116.
223 TNA, HO 107/594/23.
224 British Red Cross, *List of Auxiliary Hospitals in the UK during the First World War* (n.d., *c*.2013), 25.
225 *Domesday*, 632.

this the third largest of 289 Leicestershire towns and villages for which returns survive,[226] and the population may have been higher still before the Black Death. Contraction is seen by 1400, when potential manorial income was reduced by 104*s*. 11½*d*. through rent reductions and lack of tenants.[227] Empty plots were still recorded in 1462,[228] and in 1563, there were only 70 resident households.[229] Plague struck in August 1579, killing 63 residents in four months,[230] but there appears to have been a sharp recovery in a period when England's population also rose rapidly, with 380 communicants enumerated in 1603,[231] and 150 households in 1670,[232] perhaps 675 inhabitants. There were presentments at Donington's manor courts in the 1660s and 1670s for dividing cottages and building new ones,[233] but reliance cannot be placed on vicar George Gell's report of 200 families in the parish in 1706, a suspiciously round figure which he reduced to 150 just three years later.[234]

The 1801 census provides a firm figure of 1,959 inhabitants, rising to 3,508 in 1841. The collapse of the lace trade led to migration and emigration, and numbers declined to 2,445 in 1861,[235] with 200 houses and some shops reported empty in 1863.[236] The population remained stable at this lower level until after the Second World War. Growth followed peace, with the population exceeding 3,000 in 1951 for the first time in a century.[237] From 3,563 in 1961, there was a large increase to 5,100 in 1971, and after further growth the population in 2011 was 6,416.[238]

226 *Poll Taxes 1377–81* (ed.) Fenwick, I, 484–91.

227 TNA, DL 29/728/11987.

228 TNA, DL 43/6/3.

229 A. Dyer and D.M. Palliser (eds), *The Diocesan Population Returns for 1563 and 1603* (Oxford, 2005), 224.

230 Par. registers.

231 Dyer and Palliser, *Diocesan Population,* 376; due to document damage only the initial digit is clear.

232 *VCH Leics.* III, 171.

233 Town bk, especially 1666 and 1674.

234 J. Broad (ed.), *Bishop Wake's Summary of Visitation Returns from the Diocese of Lincoln 1705–15,* II (Oxford, 2012), 735–6.

235 *VCH Leics.* III, 187, 205.

236 W. White, *Dir. Leics. and Rutl.* (Sheffield, 1863), 483.

237 *VCH Leics.* III, 187.

238 Census, 1961–2011.

LANDOWNERSHIP

DONINGTON APPEARS TO HAVE been a place of some importance in the late Saxon period with land held by both King Harold and Aelfgifu, countess of Mercia. These holdings were merged by the early 12th century, and Donington became a distant satellite of the estates of the constables of Chester, who were instrumental in creating the medieval town. Through inheritance and marriage, the manor passed to Thomas, earl of Lancaster in 1311, and by 1400 had passed to the duchy of Lancaster. The sale of Donington Park in 1595 to Sir George Hastings created a large estate within the parish. The manor was sold by the Duchy in 1628, and bought by Sir John Coke and his son of Melbourne Hall in 1633, whose descendants held it into the 21st century.

The estates of the hospital, vicarage and chantries held little land in the Middle Ages. Norton Priory held *c*.180 a. together with the church and great tithes, and these passed through several hands after the dissolution. The great tithes were converted to over 220 a. at parliamentary inclosure in 1779, but this landholding had been divided and sold by 1831, leaving Donington Park as the only significant estate in the parish. This was divided in the 20th century, creating three separate estates of Hall, motor-racing circuit and parkland.

The Manor

Aelfgifu, countess of Mercia, held 22½ carucates of land in Donington in 1066 (*c*.2,700 a.), together with woodland of 12 by 8 furlongs (*c*.670 a.) and a mill.[1] A further five carucates (*c*.600 a.) and a meadow of unknown size were held by King Harold, as part of his manor of Barrow upon Soar.[2] The parish anciently included both banks of the river, and it is possible that Donington was part of a large estate extending across the Trent, as Weston-on-Trent (Derb.) with its berewicks was held by Earl Aelfgar in 1066.[3]

In 1086, King Harold's land was held by Hugh, earl of Chester, King William's nephew, and it is possible that he also held the countess's land, where Domesday Book is silent. Only 22½ carucates were recorded in Donington 'with appendages' in 1130, held by the earl of Chester.[4] No second manor was mentioned, and the two holdings may have been merged, perhaps with some land recorded within Diseworth, which had 3 carucates in 1086, but 9½ in 1130,[5] or Hemington, as neither Hemington nor Lockington are recorded in 1086.

1   *Domesday*, 632.
2   Ibid., 648.
3   *Domesday*, 743.
4   C.F. Slade, *The Leicestershire Survey, c.A.D. 1130* (Leicester, 1956), 18.
5   Ibid., 19, 46; *Domesday, 643.*

By 1134 the earl had granted the manor of Donington to his barons of Halton, and it remained with that family until 1322, passing from William FitzNigel (d. *c*.1134) to his son William FitzWilliam (d. *c*.1150), who was succeeded as baron by his sister's husband Eustace FitzJohn (d. 1157),[6] reputed to have built Donington's castle. Manor and castle passed by inheritance to their son Richard FitzEustace (d. 1163), and his son John FitzRichard (d. 1190).[7] John's son Roger (d. 1211) inherited, and also received the honor of Pontefract from his grandmother in 1194, taking the name de Lacy.[8] After Roger's death, Donington manor passed to his son John, a member of the baronial council following the sealing of Magna Carta in 1215.[9] He was pardoned by Henry III for his part in the barons' war,[10] and created Earl of Lincoln in 1232.[11] On his death in 1240, the manor passed to his son Edmund (d. 1258),[12] and then to Edmund's son Henry (d. 1311).[13]

With no surviving sons, after Henry's death the manor passed to his daughter Alice, countess of Salisbury and Lincoln, and wife of Thomas, earl of Lancaster and Leicester.[14] Lancaster rebelled against his cousin King Edward II, but surrendered in 1322, and was executed.[15] Donington was granted to Hugh Despenser the younger,[16] who almost immediately transferred it to his father, Hugh Despenser, earl of Winchester.[17] Both Despensers were executed in 1326 prior to the deposition of Edward II.[18] Donington was granted to Edmund, earl of Kent in 1327.[19] Edmund was executed in 1330 for allegedly trying to restore Edward II,[20] and the manor was granted to Geoffrey Mortimer,[21] son of Roger Mortimer, earl of March and de facto regent for the young Edward III. Following Edward III's successful coup against Mortimer, Edmund's widow Margaret successfully petitioned for the attainder against her husband to be removed, and Donington was restored to their son, also Edmund (d. 1331).[22] He was succeeded by his brother John (d. 1352),[23] and then their sister Joan, the so-called 'Fair Maid of Kent' (d. 1385).[24] She married first Thomas Holland (d. 1360) and, after his death, Edward of Woodstock, the

6   W. Beamont, *A History of the Castle of Halton* (Warrington, 1873), 11.

7   *Complete Peerage*, vii, 677.

8   *Complete Peerage*, vii, 677; *ODNB*, s.v. 'Lacy, Roger de (d. 1211), soldier and administrator', accessed 6 Jul. 2014.

9   *ODNB*, s.v. 'Lacy, John de, third earl of Lincoln (*c*.1192–1240)', accessed 22 Jul. 2014.

10   *Complete Peerage*, vii, 678.

11   Ibid., 675–6.

12   Ibid., 679–80; *Cal. Pat.* 1247–58, 14.

13   *Cal. Pat.* 1247–58, 649; *Cal. Pat.* 1258–66, 12; *Complete Peerage,* vii, 681.

14   *Cal. Inq. p.m.* V, p. 156; *Complete Peerage*, vii, 687; xi, 384.

15   *ODNB*, s.v. 'Thomas of Lancaster, second earl of Lancaster, second earl of Leicester, and earl of Lincoln', accessed 20 Jul. 2013.

16   *Cal Pat.* 1321–24, 191; *Cal. Chart.* 1300–26, 449.

17   *Cal. Pat.* 1324–7, 102.

18   *ODNB*, s.v. 'Despenser, Hugh, the elder, earl of Winchester (1261–1326)'; 'Despenser, Hugh, the younger, first Lord Despenser (*d.* 1326)', both accessed 8 Jul 2014.

19   *Cal. Pat.* 1327–30, 246; *Cal. Chart.* 1327–41, 4.

20   *Complete Peerage*, vii, 146–7; *Cal. Inq. p.m.* VII, p. 227.

21   *Cal. Chart.* 1327–41, 176.

22   *Cal. Close,* 1330–33, 205; *Complete Peerage*, vii, 148.

23   *Cal. Close,* 1346–49, 280; *Cal. Close,* 1349–54, 39–40; *Complete Peerage*, vii, 148.

24   *Cal. Inq. p.m.* X, p. 45; *Complete Peerage*, vii, 149.

Black Prince, eldest son of Edward III (d. 1376).[25] On her death the manor passed firstly to Thomas Holland (d. 1397), her eldest son from her first marriage,[26] then to Thomas's son, also Thomas.[27] He was executed in 1400 for involvement in a plot to restore Richard II.[28] Donington was initially among several manors granted by Henry IV to the Italian knight Francis de Court in February 1400,[29] but omitted from the confirmation two weeks later.[30] As a former holding of Thomas, earl of Lancaster, the judgement against whom had been set aside in 1327, Henry IV reunited Donington manor with his inheritance of Lancaster,[31] and it remained in the hands of the duchy of Lancaster until 1628.

Management under the Duchy of Lancaster

A series of stewards and constables appointed between 1400 and 1569 managed the duchy's interests. Under Henry VI the two offices were held in different hands, with the stewardship granted to his steward of the honor of Leicester.[32] Shortly after Edward IV's accession in 1461, he appointed William, Lord Hastings as both steward and constable at Donington,[33] and subsequent appointments were mostly to both offices, for life. Three of the appointees appear to have been resident: Robert Staunton (from 1485), a gentleman usher of the chamber who had been William Hastings' deputy,[34] Robert Haselrigge (from 1517), a groom of the wardrobe,[35] and Thomas Grey (from c.1538), yeoman usher and probably the grandson (through illegitimacy) of Lord Grey of Codnor.[36] In 1569 the manor was leased to Henry Knowles, together with the disposal of the offices,[37] excluding the mills and various small parcels of land, which were already let until 1591.[38] Other leases of the manor followed, including a 19-year term granted in 1591 to Edward Hastings and Francis Beaumont.[39]

Descent from 1628

Needing to raise money in 1628, the manor became one of many sold by Charles I to Sir Edward Ditchfield and others of the city of London.[40] They sold it in 1633 to secretary

---

25 *Cal. Inq. p.m.* X, p. 552; *Complete Peerage*, vii, 152-3.
26 *Cal. Inq. p.m.* XVI, p. 116; *Cal Pat.* 1396–99, 113, 140.
27 *Cal. Inq. p.m.* XVII, p. 301–2, 299.
28 Ibid., p. 158–9; XIIa, p. 512; XVIII, p. 333.
29 *Cal. Pat.* 1399–1401, 222–3.
30 Ibid., 232.
31 Ibid., 426.
32 Somerville, *History* I, 563, 572–4; H. Castor, *The King, the Crown and the Duchy of Lancaster: Public Authority and Private Power, 1399–1461* (Oxford, 2004), 28–9.
33 Somerville, *History* I, 572–3.
34 TNA, DL 42/21, f. 123; Somerville, *History* I, 572–4.
35 TNA, DL 42/22, f. 41; Somerville, *History* I, 573–4.
36 Nichols III, 863; TNA, DL 30/80/1100; Somerville, *History* I, 573–4.
37 Somerville, *History* I, 573n.
38 TNA, DL 42/44, ff. 300v–302.
39 TNA, DL 42/47 ff. 105–107.
40 S.J. Madge, *Domesday of Crown Lands* (1938), 318.

of state Sir John Coke (d. 1644) and his son John (d. 1650) of Melbourne Hall (Derb.), for £1,450.[41] The elder Coke supported the king during the Civil War and the estate was sequestered in 1643, but John II supported parliament. His brother Thomas was a Royalist who had compounded for his estates in 1648.[42] He inherited Donington manor in 1650, and died in 1656. He was succeeded by his son John (d. 1692), then John's son Thomas (d. 1727), who settled the manor and estates on his son George Lewis Coke (d. 1751),[43] all resident at Melbourne Hall. With no children to inherit, the manor then passed to George's sister Charlotte, married to Matthew Lamb of Brocket Hall, Hatfield (Herts.).[44] Their son Peniston inherited. He was elevated to the peerage as Baron (later Viscount) Melbourne, died in 1828, and was succeeded by his son William (d. 1848),[45] the first of two prime ministers to hold this manor. William had no children, but under his father's will the manor and properties passed first to his brother Frederick (d. 1853), who was also childless, then to their sister Emily.[46] She married Peter, earl Cowper, and after his death, Viscount Palmerston (Prime Minister, d. 1865).[47] Lady Palmerston died in 1869 and the manor passed to a grandson by her first marriage, Francis, 7th earl Cowper. He died in 1905 with no direct heir, and the estates were divided.[48] The manor of Castle Donington was inherited by his sister Lady Amabel Kerr, who moved to Melbourne Hall. Residual manorial rights in 2015 remained with the Kerr family.

The Castle

The castle occupies a naturally defensible site on the edge of the sandstone ridge, with a commanding view of the Trent valley, at a point where the land drops away sharply to the north and west. 'Enclosure' castles, such as this, where the principal defence comprises the walls and towers bounding the site, are rare nationally, especially in central England. Major earthworks remain, although partially backfilled.[49] The central area is almost hexagonal, 80 m. across and surrounded by a moat, 30 m. wide and 5 m. deep. A counterscarp created on the northern side provided a defensive bank 2 m. high and 5 m. wide. Part of a second outer ditch has been recut to create a modern road.[50]

The castle almost certainly predated a treaty drawn up between 1148 and 1153 by the earls of Chester and Leicester, who agreed that no new castles should be built between

41   Melb. Hall Est. Office, X94/40/1/18; X/94/58/5/28 (providing amount but quoting incorrect year).

42   *ODNB*, s.v. 'Coke, Sir John, (1563–1644), politician', accessed 15 Aug. 2014; *Cal. Cttee for Money*, I, 165–6; *Cal. Cttee Compounding*, II, 1844–9, *HMC, Cowper* II, 340–1, 342.

43   TNA, PROB 11/615/437.

44   *ODNB*, s.v. 'Lamb, Sir Matthew, first baronet (1705?–1768), politician and lawyer', accessed 15 Aug. 2014.

45   *ODNB*, s.v. 'Lamb, William, second Viscount Melbourne', accessed 15 Aug. 2014.

46   TNA, PROB 11/1748/97; PROB 11/2090/68.

47   *ODNB*, s.v. 'Temple [*née* Lamb], Emily Mary', accessed 15 Aug. 2014.

48   *ODNB*, s.v. 'Cowper, Francis Thomas de Grey, seventh Earl Cowper (1834–1905), politician and landowner', accessed 15 Aug. 2014.

49   NHL, no. 1011608, Enclosure Castle at Donington, accessed 22 Mar. 2016.

50   B.W. Hodgkinson, 'The East Midlands earthwork project: Castle Donington' (Univ. of Nottingham, unpub., undated), copy at Leics. County Hall.

Figure 6 *Sketch of 1792, showing the castle earthworks and part of the medieval walls, with later thatched cottages.*

Coventry and Donington, or between Donington and Leicester.[51] Tradition attributes its building to Eustace FitzJohn,[52] who held the manor between *c*.1150 and 1157. The William FitzNigel who negotiated this treaty on behalf of the Earl of Chester is unlikely to be the Baron Halton of that name, who died more than a decade before the treaty was concluded. When John de Lacy inherited in 1213, the castle was retained by King John as security against rebellion.[53] It was released in 1214,[54] but the king ordered its destruction in 1216,[55] although the order may not have been executed, due to the king's death. It was given to the sheriff to imprison hostages in 1242,[56] and delivered to Adam de Gesemuth in 1266, 'for the defence of these parts',[57] suggesting a functioning building. The combination of an absent lord and population pressures resulted in tenant plots overlaying its ditch by 1303,[58] but Thomas, earl of Lancaster sealed documents at Castle Donington in 1314–15,[59] and a household was resident during the earl's rebellion in 1322, when the king's soldiers broke down doors and took away locks.[60] It may have been abandoned shortly thereafter, as the buildings were said to be 'weak and ruinous' in 1331.[61]

51   *VCH Leics.*, II, 80.
52   Burton, 83; Nichols III, 770.
53   *Rot. Lit. Claus.* I, 151.
54   *Rot. Lit. Claus.* I, 169.
55   *Rot. Lit. Claus.* I, 251.
56   *Cal. Close 1237–4* , 442.
57   *Cal. Pat. 1258–66*, 597.
58   TNA, DL 25/1205; DL 25/1772.
59   TNA, DL 25/3446, DL 25/1858, DL 25/2294, DL 25/1467, DL 25/3332.
60   TNA, SC 6/1146/9 m. 3; Fox, 244-5, 270.
61   TNA, C 135/24/30.

The duchy of Lancaster set stone cutters and carpenters to work on repairs in 1409,[62] but by 1564 there was only a 'house' of stud and plaster in the yard, a tower converted into a dovecote, and stone which was being taken by steward Thomas Grey for his new house at Langley.[63] Further stone was taken without authority and sold outside the parish by Thomas and John Bentley in 1674.[64] In 1792, some rough walling survived, including a round-headed doorway, perhaps of the 12th century (Fig. 6).[65] The medieval walls were largely demolished in the early 20th century, when a new house was built on the site,[66] but a small section survived in situ in 1997.[67]

Derby Hills

Upland grazing of *c*.300 a. known as Derby Hills, 5 miles from Donington, was attached to the manor. This appears to have originated as part of a large area of common grazing available to Repton abbey (Derb.) and the tenants of Melbourne, Ingleby, Foremark, Ticknall, Calke (all Derb.) and Castle Donington.[68] The land is difficult to identify in most manorial accounts, but rent of £1 3s. 7½d. received in 1322 for 99¾ a. of 'waste' in Ticknall and 'Bollehaghe' (possibly Bolkley Gate) almost certainly relates to Derby Hills, and a further 5 a. had been inclosed by the prior of Repton but subsequently taken by Melbourne residents, who claimed it as their common.[69] By 1513, Richard Fraunces of Ticknall had inclosed further land.[70] All the land appears to have been apportioned between the various manors by 1640, with the area known as Derby Hills being exclusively for Donington's copyholders.[71]

Sir John Coke inclosed the land in 1638, but his fences were set alight in 1640.[72] The land was finally inclosed by an Act of 1770,[73] when Lord Melbourne was awarded 223 a. 0 r. 28 p.,[74] in addition to 23 a. 1 r. 22 p. he had already inclosed. A residual 30 a. was allotted to 51 tenants.[75]

62   *Cal. Pat.* 1408–13, 108.
63   TNA, DL 44/105.
64   Town bk, 1674.
65   ROLLR, 'Grangerised' Nichols, III, facing 781.
66   ROLLR, DE 5D 33/184, Castle Donington, letter 4 Dec. 1925.
67   Ryder, (1997), 2, 41.
68   TNA, DL 42/95, f. 32.
69   TNA, SC6/1146/9, m. 3; Fox, 244.
70   TNA, DL 42/95, f. 32.
71   TNA, DL 4/98/28.
72   Melb. Hall Est. Office, X94/58/3/1–5, X94/58/6/36.
73   10 Geo. III, c. 13.
74   Derb. RO, Q/RI 34.
75   Melb. Hall Est. Office, X94/P/1/14.

Donington Park

Origins of the Park Estate

Donington Park was probably created shortly before 1229, and was extended in 1483 and c.1550.[76] It was part of the manor until 1595, but its existence as a separate estate can be traced to 1539, when Duchy steward Robert Haselrigge and his deputy were said to have had two lodges in the park, each with two hearths.[77] Haselrigge's successor Thomas Grey described himself 'of Castell Donyngton parke' in 1565.[78] A lodge was said to be ruinous in 1571,[79] and in 1591 the queen authorised 16 trees to be taken from Derby Hills for its repair.[80]

Park Estate from 1590

Sir George Hastings took a 41-year lease of the park in 1590.[81] It was sold in 1595 to Robert Devereux, earl of Essex, who sold it four months later for £3,000 to Sir George Hastings,[82] soon to become the 4th earl of Huntingdon. In 1601, the earl took a 31-year lease of Ramsley Wood in Melbourne, on the western edge of the park.[83] On the 4th earl's death in 1604, the estate was inherited by his grandson Henry, a minor (d. 1643).[84] Although the estate was severely impoverished, and land elsewhere was sold,[85] Henry's trustees consolidated their local interests through the purchase of the manor of Melbourne in 1605.[86] After Henry's death, his son Ferdinando, 6th earl (d. 1656), inherited, and Donington Park became the main home of the family following the surrender of Ashby castle to parliament in 1646.[87]

The estate passed from Ferdinando to his son Theophilus, 7th earl (d. 1701). In 1675, Theophilus purchased 61 a. known as Melbourne Coppice, Short Stocking and Ramsley Flatts from George Grey, and inclosed part of this land 'in the north-west corner' of the park.[88] This portion was presumably the 'Ridings', which Grey's grandfather had been accused of taking from Anne Haselrigge in 1554,[89] and which the manor court heard in

---

76   Below, 50–3.
77   TNA, DL 3/31/G1; P. Liddle, 'A late medieval enclosure in Donington Park', *Trans. LAHS,* 53 (1977-8), 8–29.
78   TNA, PROB 11/48/274.
79   TNA, DL 42/99, f. 5 and 5v.
80   TNA, DL 42/98, ff. 91v, 101v–102.
81   TNA, DL 42/47, ff. 100–104v.
82   ROLLR, DE362/S/Temp1, p. 24.
83   ROLLR, DE362/S/Temp1, p. 8.
84   *Complete Peerage,* VI, 657–8.
85   *ODNB,* s.v. 'Hastings, Henry, 5th earl of Huntingdon (1586–1643), nobleman and landowner' (accessed 18 Mar. 2016).
86   ROLLR, DE362/S/Temp1, p. 8.
87   *Cal. SP Dom.,* 1645–7, 342, 252, 356–7.
88   ROLLR, DE362/S/Temp1, pp. 12–13.
89   TNA, DL 3/81/C4.

1675 had recently been 'locked up'.[90] Part of the Flatts were in Melbourne parish, near the shire mere (boundary).[91] The remaining land may have comprised all or most of the western extension of the park beyond the prominent early boundary bank and ditch into Melbourne parish (Map 9).

Theophilus's eldest son George (d. 1705) inherited the earldom, but the estate was settled on his second son, also Theophilus (d. 1746),[92] who became the 9th earl on the death of his half-brother. His heir was his son Francis, 10th earl, who died unmarried in 1789. Francis bequeathed his lands to his nephew Francis, Lord Rawdon, 2nd earl of Moira from 1793 and marquis of Hastings from 1817.[93] Lord Rawdon commissioned a new mansion, completed in 1793. In 1804 he married Flora, the only daughter and heir of the 5th earl of Loudoun, bringing another title and a Scottish estate into the family.[94] On the death of Francis in 1826, the estate passed to his son George (d. 1844), then from George first to his son Paulyn (d. 1851),[95] and then to Paulyn's brother Henry, aged only eight on his brother's death.[96] When Henry came of age he 'acted as if [horse] racing had been invented for no other purpose than to dissipate wealth'.[97] He died in poor health and with ruined finances at the age of just 26 in 1868, married but childless.[98] Many of the contents of the Hall had to be sold to clear his debts,[99] but his sister Edith's husband, Charles Frederick Clifton, who had taken the name Abney-Hastings in 1859, bought the reversion of the English estates.[100] Edith died in 1874; a monument in the park overlooking the Trent, in the form of a Celtic cross surrounded by boulders grouped in the shape of a hand, is said to mark where her right hand was buried to keep watch on the estate;[101] the remainder of her body was laid to rest in a family vault in Scotland.[102] Her widower was created Baron Donington in 1880, and lived at Donington Hall until his death in 1895.[103] His son Charles (11th earl of Loudoun) inherited.[104]

The Hall and park were purchased by private treaty in 1903 by Major Frederick Gretton,[105] whose late father had been a director of the brewers Bass, Ratcliff and Gretton.[106] On his death in 1928, the estate passed to his older brother Colonel John Gretton of Stapleford Park, who almost immediately placed it on the market;[107] agent's details quoted an annual income of £2,570, including fishing (leased from the lord of the

90   Town bk.
91   TNA, DL 1/118/T5.
92   TNA, PROB 11/460/381.
93   TNA, PROB 11/1184/78; *Complete Peerage*, ix, 29–31.
94   *Complete Peerage*, viii, 162–3.
95   *Complete Peerage*, vi, 379.
96   Ibid., 379–80.
97   *The Times*, 11 Nov. 1868, 9.
98   Ibid., 12 Nov. 1868, 10; *Complete Peerage*, vi, 380.
99   *The Times*, 21 Dec. 1868, 16; 16 Jan.1869, 5; 26 Feb. 1869, 10; 8 Mar. 1869, 3; 30 Jun. 1869, 8.
100 *Complete Peerage*, viii, 164.
101 NHL, no. 1361332, The Countess Cross: accessed 30 Apr. 2016.
102 *Country Life*, 29 Apr. 1971, 00.
103 *Complete Peerage*, iv, 399.
104 *Complete Peerage*, viii, 165.
105 *Derby Daily Telegraph*, 5 Jun. 1903.
106 *Grantham Jnl*, 14 Oct. 1899.
107 *Derby Daily Telegraph*, 30 Nov. 1928; Derb. RO, D302 Z/ES 50.

manor) and shooting.[108] It was purchased by E.W.S. Bartlett, a timber merchant of Exeter, who accepted an offer for the estate in 1929 from John Gillies Shields of Isley Walton.[109] Shields had moved to England from Scotland in 1882 as land agent to Lord Donington, and had served the 1st and 2nd barons Donington and also Major Gretton in this capacity, alongside developing his own business, Breedon and Cloud Hill Lime Works.[110]

From 1930 the hall was converted to a country-club hotel, with a golf course, tennis courts and a boating marina on the river.[111] The motor racing circuit was constructed in 1931,[112] but the site was commandeered by the army in 1939, and used as a vehicle depot.[113] Car and motorcycle manufacturers sought its release in 1946 to aid exports, as it was the only track suitable for vehicle testing,[114] but the army remained until 1956.[115] Shields died in 1943, and had bequeathed the estate to his grandson, also J.G. Shields, a serving army officer.[116] It was divided in the later 20th century. The racetrack was sold in 1971 to F.B. (Tom) Wheatcroft,[117] and the Hall was sold to British Midland Airways (later BMI) in 1980,[118] serving as their headquarters until 1982.[119] In 2013, the Hall and the neighbouring Hastings House (offices built by BMI) were purchased by Norton Motorcycles, previously based at the racetrack.[120]

The deer herd was rebuilt after the army left in 1956. The core area of the deer park (38.9 ha.) was designated a Site of Special Scientific Interest in 1983,[121] and in 2015 was managed under the Countryside Stewardship Scheme. The deer park and farmland were still held by the Shields family in 2015, when around 300 deer grazed on *c.*160 a. (65 ha.).[122]

Donington Hall

Little is known about the buildings in the park before 1790. Sir George Hastings reputedly took stone from the castle from 1595 to build a modest house,[123] and signed letters in 1602 and 1603 from 'my lodge in Donington Park'.[124] Although the family's main home was 10 miles away at Ashby-de-la-Zouch, the 5th earl also signed many letters from Donington between 1624 and 1640.[125] Further buildings were added in 1643

---

108 *The Times*, 10 Jan. 1929.

109 *Dundee Courier*, 19 Apr. 1929.

110 ROLLR, DE 500/150/9; *Derby Daily Telegraph*, 19 Apr. 1929, 21 Aug. 1936, 12 May 1943.

111 J.G. Shields, 'A refuge of two centuries', *Country Life*, 22 Mar. 1979, 828–30.

112 *Derby Daily Telegraph*, 24 Apr. 1931.

113 152 *HL Deb*. 5th ser. 929–30.

114 420 *HC Deb*. 5th ser. 1240–50.

115 *The Times*, 4 Aug. 1956.

116 J.G. Shields, 'A refuge of two centuries', *Country Life*, 22 Mar. 1979, 828–30.

117 http://www.donington-park.co.uk/about-donington/tom-wheatcroft/ (accessed 24 Sept. 2014)

118 P. Olsen, *Donington Hall: The History of an Ancient Family Seat* (Cambridge, 1990), 49–50; B. Gunston, *Diamond Flight: The Story of British Midland* (1988), 81–2.

119 *Derby Telegraph*, 12 Mar. 2013, 16 Mar. 2013.

120 Ibid., 16 Mar. 2013, 10 Apr. 2013.

121 https://designatedsites.naturalengland.org.uk (accessed 24 Aug. 2014).

122 http://www.parkfarmhouse.co.uk/history-of-the-deer-park/ (accessed 18 Mar. 2016).

123 Burton, 89.

124 *HMC Salisbury XII*, 119, 663.

125 *Cal. SP Dom. 1623–5, 329; 1627–8, 50, 68, 193, 215, 424, 540; 1631–3, 521; 1640, 340, 435, 455;* Huntington Libr., HAM 53/6, ff. 164–177v.

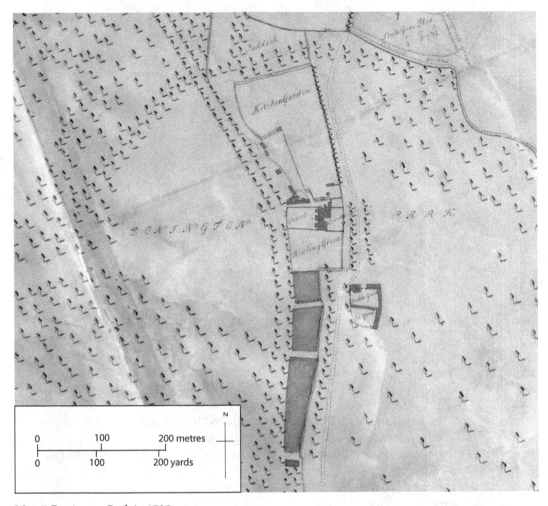

Map 7 *Donington Park in 1735.*

under an agreement for John Chapman to 'make readie in Donington Parke' 100,000 bricks, at a price of 5s. per 1,000.[126] Donington became the main family home after Ashby Castle was surrendered to parliamentary troops and slighted in 1646.[127] It was an extensive property, with 40 hearths in 1664, after three had been 'pulld downe'.[128] A plan of 1735 shows a large house with courtyards east and west, standing in wooded parkland, a smaller building to the north-west, with outbuildings and a walled kitchen garden beyond. To the south are a bowling green, stables, a livestock yard and series of what

126 A Mc Whirr, 'Brickmaking in Leicestershire before 1710', *Trans. LAHS*, 71 (1997) 55, incorporated a transcript from Huntington Libr., Hastings Deeds 73/392–401.

127 *Cal. S.P. Dom.,* 1645–7, 342, 252, 356–7.

128 TNA, E 179/251/4.

Figure 7 *Humphrey Repton's watercolour of the first mansion in Donington Park.*

are probably ponds (Map 7).[129] Further buildings were added in 1755–6,[130] resulting in a 'patchwork of different periods, blazoned over with a disgusting yellow colour' (Fig. 7).[131] A visitor in 1789 'took it for a gardeners, or some lodge' and 'of the worst taste'.[132]

Shortly after inheriting the estate from his uncle in 1789, the 2nd earl of Moira replaced this range of buildings with a single imposing property. Humphrey Repton produced two 'moveable views' in 1790, and introduced William Wilkins (senior) to design the Hall.[133] It was built on the site of its predecessor, where three valleys met.[134] The exterior of the new house was in the Gothic style, with a large entrance porch on the south and four wings arranged around a central courtyard. Built in ashlar, with plaster decoration and a carved inscription over the entrance dedicating the building to the memory of the 10th earl, Wilkins' corner turrets were omitted from the final design, and a Gothic chapel was added to the east. A fanlight over the entrance contains heraldic glass by the Irish artist Richard Hand.[135] The interior is classical. The plan was published in *The New Vitruvius Britannicus,* and influenced several other properties, including Coleorton Hall and Belvoir Castle in Leicestershire, Sezincote (Gloucs.) and Highclere (Hants.).[136] It has been assumed that the landscaping of the park was by Repton,[137] although no 'Red Book' was produced and Repton hardly mentions Donington in his own publications. Comparison of plans of 1735 and 1833 show additional woodland

129 ROLLR, DG 30/Ma/64/2.
130 *HMC Hastings, III,* 23, 100, 105, 118.
131 *Topographer for the year 1789,* 86; ROLLR, 'Grangerised' Nichols III, 778.
132 J. Byng (C.B. Andrews, ed.), *The Torrington Diaries,* II (1935), 75–6.
133 D. Stroud, *Humphrey Repton* (1962), 50–51; Pevsner, 125; the 'moveable views' are at ROLLR, Grangerised Nichols III, 778.
134 J. Britton, *The Beauties of England and Wales,* IX (1807), 399.
135 Pevsner, 127.
136 G. Richardson, *New Vitruvius Britannicus,* (1808), II, 31–35; J. Brushe, 'Wilkins Senior's original designs for Donington Park as proposed by Repton', *Burlington Mag.,* 121 (1979), 113–4. There is a plan of the ground floor in Pevsner, 126.
137 Pevsner, 125.

had been planted to the south of the Hall, the ponds and some avenues of trees had been removed, a new lake created north of the Hall, and there had been substantial landscaping work near the park's northern boundary.[138] Later changes, including caves and a waterfall, may be the work of James Pulham and Son in 1866–7.[139]

The Hall was requisitioned as a prisoner-of-war camp for 320 German officers and 80 servants in 1915, leading to questions in parliament about the relative standards of accommodation of the British Army and the German prisoners, and a visit by MPs.[140] Six prisoners escaped, one of whom (Gunther Plüschow) evaded capture and successfully returned to Germany.[141] It was returned to Mr Shields after the war, but taken over by the army in 1939. After they left in 1956, Major Shields lent the Hall, firstly for use by Hungarian refugees, over 400 passing through before the crisis eased in 1957,[142] and then to the Ockenden Venture until 1966, as a home for displaced children.[143]

Religious Estates

Norton Priory

By 1134, William FitzNigel had given one carucate of land in Donington (*c*.120 a.), half a carucate in Wavertoft (west of Diseworth), Donington church and the tithes of Donington mill to his Augustinian foundation of Runcorn (later Norton) priory, in Cheshire.[144] The priory had probably built a grange on the Wavertoft land by 1247, when Robert 'le Granger de Wavertoft' is recorded.[145] Norton was raised to the status of a mitred abbey in 1391.[146]

John Parsons was Norton's farmer in 1535,[147] and Thomas Parsons senior and junior were the tenants when the rectory was sold in 1545 for £360 10s. to Robert Lawrence and William Symson.[148] The Parsons almost certainly lived on the site of a later farmhouse called Wartop Grange, adjacent to Diseworth brook, where some 'old walls' stood in 1804.[149] The confusing parochial status of the land is evident in the wills of widow Isabelle Parsons of 'Wavertoft Grange in Castle Donington' (d. 1567),[150] and yeoman Thomas Parsons of 'Wartoft Grange in Diseworth' (d. 1594).[151]

138 ROLLR, DG 30/Ma/64/2; QS 48/1/95/1.

139 http://www.pastscape.org.uk/hob.aspx?hob_id=315352.

140 70 *Parl. Debates* 3rd ser. 248–51, 380–1, 557–9, 968–70, 1137–40; 71 *Parl. Debates* 3rd ser., 388–93; 82 *Parl. Deb.* 3rd ser., 2554–6; *The Times*, 6 Mar. 1915; 9 Mar. 1915.

141 *Derby Daily Telegraph*, 4 Oct. 1915, 19 Jul. 1917, 22 Jun. 1922.

142 *The Times*, 19 Nov. 1956.

143 TNA, BN 62/3145.

144 J. Tait (ed.), 'The foundation charter of Runcorn (later Norton) priory' (Chetham Society, n.s. 100, Manchester, 1939), 19–20; *Cal. Chart. 1327–41*, 124; *VCH Ches.* III, 165.

145 W. Dugdale (ed. J. Caley), *Monasticon Anglicanum* (1830), IV, 223.

146 J.P. Greene, *Norton Priory: The Archaeology of a Medieval Religious House* (Cambridge, 1989), 65–6.

147 *Valor Eccl.*, V, 210.

148 *L & P Hen. VIII*, XX, (2), p. 216; *HMC Hastings I*, p. 35.

149 Nichols, III, 785.

150 ROLLR, Will Reg. 1567/5.

151 ROLLR, Wills & Inventories file 1594/86.

The Wavertoft land changed hands with the great tithes and advowson until 1649. Lawrence and Symson sold them to John Beaumont, the surveyor of monasteries for Thomas Cromwell in 1545,[152] but after confessing to peculation in 1552 while Receiver of the Court of Wards, Beaumont's Leicestershire property was granted in 1553 to Francis, 2nd earl of Huntingdon (d. 1560).[153] They passed to the 3rd earl,[154] who sold them in 1588 to Humphrey Adderley of Weddington (Warws.). Adderley's son, also Humphrey, sold them in 1619 to Sir Edward (later baron) Montague, who settled them on John Manners (later 8th earl of Rutland) upon marriage to his daughter Frances in 1628.[155] The Wavertoft land was separated from the rectory and advowson in 1649, when it was sold to Joseph Kniveton of Diseworth for £2,200.[156] By 1678, Kniveton had sold half to an unknown party.[157] Kniveton was regularly amerced at the manor court for trespass with livestock on stinted pastures, and it was recorded in 1669 that the 'Antient Grange House' only had rights of common for ten cows and one bull in Stonehill Field as far as Leicester Way after harvest, and 80 sheep when that field was fallow.[158] Subsequent owners of the Wavertoft site include Richard Cheslyn, whose 'old inclosures' totalled 46 a. 3 r. 27 p. in 1799.[159] The land was still held by the Cheslyn family in 1831,[160] and probably later acquired by the Shakespeare family, who bought Cheslyn's property at Langley.

Wavertoft was considered to be an extra-parochial area in the late 18th century, containing 130 a.,[161] far larger than the site given to Norton priory. It had been included within Castle Donington parish by 1883,[162] but was transferred to Isley-cum-Langley parish in 1936.

St John's Hospital

The hospital is believed to have been founded and endowed by John FitzRichard, 6th baron Halton (d. 1190), and was for 13 brothers and sisters who lived under no rule.[163] The dedication was variously recorded as St John, St John the Baptist,[164] and St John the Evangelist.[165] The buildings stood on a low-lying site of c.10 a. with a spring, and with a sandstone escarpment to the south, known in 1322 as 'le Spittelcliffe'.[166] It was endowed with a tithe of the demesne corn after the rector's tithe had been taken, and a tithe of the demesne hay.[167] No evidence of any subsequent endowment has been found, but by 1311

152 *L. & P. Hen. VIII*, XX, (2), p. 231.
153 *Cal. Pat. Edw. VI*, V, 228.
154 C. Cross, *The Puritan Earl: The Life of Henry Hastings, Third Earl of Huntingdon, 1536–1595* (1966), 136.
155 ROLLR, 4D 42/34.
156 Nichols, III, 785.
157 Town bk, 1678.
158 Town bk, for example, 1669, 1674, 1675, 1678.
159 Huntington Libr., HAM 9/4.
160 ROLLR, DE 253a (ii).
161 Nichols, III, 785.
162 OS map 6", Leics. X.SW (1883 edn).
163 W.P.W. Phillimore (ed.), *Rotuli Hugonis de Welles*, I, 252; *VCH Leics.*, II, 39.
164 *Cal. Close*, 1237–42, 223 (1240); TNA, DL 43/6/3 (1462); A. Hamilton Thompson, 'The Chantry Certificates for Leicestershire', *Assoc. Archit. Soc. Rep. & Papers*, 30 (1909–10), 505 (1547).
165 A.C. Wood (ed.), *Registrum Simonis Langham, Cantuariensis archiepiscopi* (Cant. & York Soc., 53, 1956), 55.
166 TNA, SC 6/1146/9, m. 3; Fox, 242.
167 Phillimore (ed.), *Rotuli Hugonis de Welles*, I, 252; *VCH Leics.*, II, 39.

the hospital also held one messuage, three bovates of land (*c*.45 a.), the tithes of the mills, and pasture for cattle in the park, in return for finding a chaplain to celebrate divine service at the castle.[168] This provided income of £2 11*s*. 6*d*. in 1291,[169] reducing to three marks (£2) in 1366,[170] but recovering to £3 13*s*. 4*d*. by 1535.[171]

When dissolved in 1547, the hospital held 3 a. of land called 'le springe', a capital messuage with two closes totalling 7 a., 10 a. of arable land in Donington's fields, and 37 a. in Nottinghamshire. It received rent from the tenants of lands called Reddam Lands,[172] which may have replaced the 'reddine tithe' on the demesne land. Thomas Brende, a London scrivener, purchased the buildings and land in 1548.[173] These were acquired by John Beaumont, and subsequently granted to the 2nd earl of Huntingdon in 1553.[174] The earl agreed a lease to Edward Edmundson in 1564 for 21 years at an annual rent of £3. The following year Edmundson assigned his remaining term to John Campion,[175] who in 1575 purchased the site, buildings and most of its land in Donington from the 3rd earl for £66 13*s*. 4*d*.[176] A residual 8 a. of arable land, meadow and pasture was sold by the earl in 1576 to Thomas Carver of Isley Walton for £8.[177]

The inclosure map of 1779 shows a large site owned by the trustees of (a later) John Campion deceased, who were allotted 6 a. 0 r. 31 p. of pasture near Cavendish Bridge and further pasture of 18 a. 0 r. 16 p. alongside the hospital, including 4 a. 0 r. 32 p. in lieu of the ancient 'reddine' tithe.[178] The remaining hospital buildings, comprising a messuage, cottage and outbuildings on a site of 9 a., together with two pieces of pasture matching the 1779 allotments, were put on the market in 1793.[179] In 1794, John Williams, a gentleman of London, purchased the 'spittle house', two cottages and 9 a. of land on 'Spittle Lane', and 26a. of other land in the parish from Campion's heir, William Needham.[180] Shortly afterwards the land is said to have been divided and sold.[181] Samuel Follows paid 5*s*. 8*d*. tax in 1796 for land described as 'late Campion',[182] but this was for only part of the former estate, for which land tax of £1 7*s*. 10½ *d*. had been paid in 1791.

A sketch of the remaining buildings in 1792 (Fig. 8) shows two ranges set at right angles, each with round-headed doorways, one (probably the chapel), with triple lancet windows perhaps of the 13th century.[183] They look a little sturdier than described in 1790, when a visitor considered the chapel 'a ruin' and was 'fearful it might fall upon

168 *Cal. Inq. p.m.*, V, p. 156.
169 *Tax. Eccl.* 67, 74.
170 Wood (ed.), *Registrum Simonis*, 55.
171 *Valor Eccl.*, IV, 179.
172 *Cal. Pat.* Edw. VI, II, 71; Hamilton Thompson, 'The Chantry Certificates', 534–5.
173 Hamilton Thompson, 'The Chantry Certificates', 535n.
174 *Cal. Pat.* Edw. VI, V, 228.
175 ROLLR, 5D 33/210/f/6/1.
176 Huntington Libr., HAD 578; Cross, *The Puritan Earl*, 310.
177 CADMT, 2015.12.1.
178 ROLLR, DE 5251/1–2.
179 *Derby Merc.*, 7 Mar. 1793.
180 Indenture: http://www.familychest.co.uk/FamilyChestDocs/documents/0503061.htm (accessed 25 Nov. 2015).
181 Nichols, III, 780.
182 ROLLR, QS 62/71.
183 ROLLR, 'Grangerised' Nichols, III, facing 781.

Figure 8 *Sketch of the hospital in 1792.*

me'.[184] Some damage may have been caused in the Civil War, as musket balls have been found in neighbouring gardens.[185] Little remained in 1863 except earthworks,[186] including fish ponds overlaying earlier ridge and furrow.[187] The site was purchased by the parish council, and levelled for a recreation ground in the 1970s.[188]

184 J. Throsby, *The supplementary volume to the Leicestershire views: containing a series of excursions in the year 1790, to the villages and places of note in the county* (London, 1790), 188–9.
185 Castle Donington Local Hist. Soc., 'An excavation of part of the mediaeval hospital of St John, Castle Donington, 1980–83' (unpubl.), copy at Leics. County Hall.
186 W. White, *Dir. Leics. and Rutl.* (Sheffield, 1863), 484.
187 R.F. Hartley, *The Medieval Earthworks of North-West Leicestershire* (Leicester, 1984), 17.
188 Castle Donington Local Hist. Soc., 'An excavation of part of the mediaeval hospital of St John, Castle Donington, 1980–83', (unpubl.), copy at Leics. County Hall.

ECONOMIC HISTORY

Overview

CASTLE DONINGTON BENEFITED FROM ITS LOCATION on a major river, where profitable fisheries, ferries and mills were established. The large parish included woodland, osier grounds, a park from 1229, and a market and fair from 1278. The manor was valued at £99 0s. 8½d. in 1311, including demesne land at £34 8s. (35 per cent) and rents and services totalling £36 8s. 1½d. (37 per cent) from 43 burgesses, 44 customary tenants with one virgate, and others. The remaining 28 per cent of the valuation included the mill (£10), foreign rents (£3), courts (£2), fishing (£2) and the market (30s.).[1]

The market and fair failed to flourish, and from the late 14th to the 18th century the economy revolved around agriculture and the benefits derived from the Trent. Some large farms developed, but these were copyhold. Of 37 people assessed for tax in 1524, only two were assessed on land, paying 3s. and 2s. against the mean assessment of 3s. 1d. for those paying on goods.[2] The enfranchisement of copyholders from the 1640s to facilitate the lord's inclosure of common land at Derby Hills gave many people a small interest in the inclosure of Donington's open fields and meadows in 1779, providing a catalyst for small-scale industrialisation. The range of occupations which developed is striking: the 88 resident freeholders who voted at the 1830 parliamentary election for Leicestershire followed 39 different trades or occupations.[3]

The collapse of the lace and knitting industries in the mid 19th century resulted in poverty and outward migration. Some urban pretensions remained, with haberdasher Mary Popple rebranding county newspapers as local editions: the *Derbyshire Chronicle* as the *Castle Donington Weekly Express* in 1858–9, the *Loughborough Monitor* as the *Castle Donington Express and Loughborough Monitor* in December 1859 and the *Derby Telegraph* as the *Castle Donington Telegraph, Leics. and Derbys. Advertiser* between 1860 and 1867.[4] By 1910, employment in the village was 'virtually nil'.[5] Little changed until 1950, when the decision to build a power station began the transformation of this village. The district and county councils encouraged commercial development from the 1960s, to offset the anticipated decline in the north-west Leicestershire coalfield, and in 1965 the opening of the airport and the M1 motorway provided the transport infrastructure

1 TNA, C 134/22/17; Farnham, 49.
2 TNA, E179/123/324, pt 1, rot. 3.
3 Poll bk, Leicestershire (1830), 48–50.
4 Lee, 'The rise and fall', 63, 79.
5 F.B. Taylor, *Dwelling in the Past: Life in Castle Donington during the 1910 to 1930 Period* (Castle Donington, 1995), 2.

to attract businesses. By the 21st century, Castle Donington had become a hub for the logistics industry, and was home to many manufacturing and service businesses.

Agriculture

Before 1483

In 1086 there were 22½ carucates of land (*c*.2,250–2,700 a.), and Donington's 15 ploughs suggest total arable of 1500–1,800 a. There had been 20 ploughs in 1066, and the reduction may indicate a greater element of pastoral farming, requiring less labour. The lord had three ploughs, suggesting 300–360 a. of arable within a demesne of *c*.450–540 a.[6] Demesne meadow of three furlongs by one furlong was held by earl Hugh, but nothing more is known about his five-carucate landholding in Donington, which formed part of a 36-carucate holding spread across 11 places .[7]

Excluding the park, created by 1229,[8] the remainder of the demesne was almost wholly arable in 1278, with no dominant cereal crop: 73 a. of wheat and 56 a. of rye grew in one field, while another contained 114 a. of oats, 20½ a. of barley and 20 a. of beans and peas. Allowing for a fallow field, this suggests total demesne arable had increased to *c*.420–450 a. Few livestock were recorded, mostly oxen and badly affected by murrain.[9] By 1311, the demesne contained 85 a. of meadow, 96 a. of pasture, and 400 a. of arable land, with the arable and pasture worth 1*s*. an acre annually, and the meadow 2*s*. per acre. Customary tenants each had to plough one acre, reap for three days, hoe for two days, and make hay for two days each year.[10] Although a populous manor, this modest level of services suggests wage labour was also employed. Some of the arable was near the Trent, and 22 a. could not be sown in 1331 'because of the inundation of the river'. A further 340 a. of demesne arable was worth just 4*d*. an acre, contrasting with 70 a. of meadow worth 2*s*. 6*d*. per acre and over 70 a. of pasture worth 10*s*. per acre.[11] If the demesne lay intermixed with other land, the peasants with their smaller landholdings would have suffered badly from the flood. The following year, 218 sheep, 17 oxen, 10 pigs and 14 horses were recorded, and 99¾ a. of 'waste' at Ticknall, which is almost certainly the land at Derby Hills.[12]

Surnames in the poll tax of 1379 suggest a largely agrarian economy.[13] Economic decline is suggested by accounts for 1400, which show a loss of 104*s*. 11½*d*. through 'reduction and decay of rents'.[14] A shortage of labour after the Black Death led to letting of the demesne, but the lords found it difficult to find tenants for large leases. A total of

6   *Domesday*, 632.
7   *Domesday*, 648.
8   *Cal. Close* 1227–31, 222.
9   Notts. Archives, DDFJ 6/1/1; D. Postles, 'The seignorial economy in N.W. Leicestershire in 1277–8', *Trans LAHS*, 52 (1976–7), 76–7, 80.
10   TNA, C 134/22/17; Farnham, 49.
11   TNA, C 135/24/30; R.H. Hilton, *Economic Development of Some Leicestershire Estates* (Oxford, 1947), 157.
12   TNA, SC6/1146/9, m. 3; Fox, 241–2.
13   *Poll Taxes 1377–81* (ed.) Fenwick I, 547–8.
14   TNA, DL 29/728/11987.

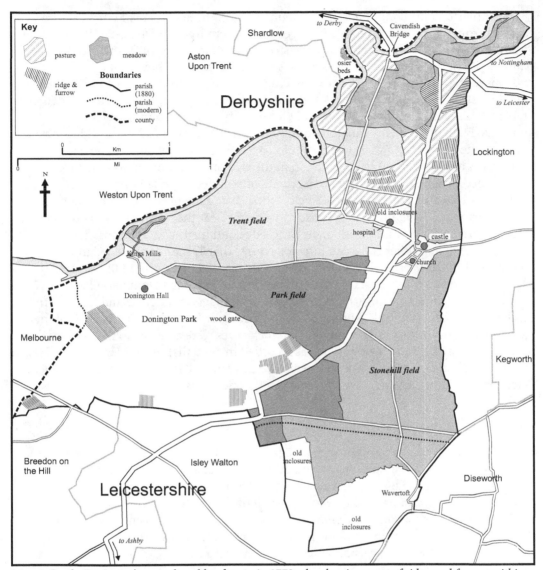

Map 8 *Castle Donington's agricultural landscape in 1778, also showing areas of ridge and furrow within the meadow, pasture and park*

206 a. 2 r. 3¾ p. was let in small parcels in 1377,[15] but in 1421 a 10-year lease of 269 a. 0 r. 30 p. arable with meadow and pasture was in place for £10 annually, with piecemeal short lets of other land, leaving less than 24 a. in the lord's hands.[16] Total rents from demesne lets varied, but £20 was not unusual. The risk of flooding remained, and £4 10s. 8d. was invested in flood defences (*garde des prees*) in 1400.[17]

15   Hilton, *Econ. Development*, 157; TNA, DL 29/183/2901.
16   Hilton 157, TNA, DL 29/183/2903.
17   TNA, DL 29/728/11987.

Wealthier tenants commuted their labour services: three holders of virgates were released from works in 1393 for payment of 2*s*. 8*d*. per virgate.[18] Demesne lets and other vacant plots enabled some to increase the size of their farms. By 1421, the manorial bailiff, William Baron, held six messuages, six virgates and one bovate of land which had lapsed to the lord, at 3*s*. 8*d*. per virgate, against the previous rent of 14*s*. 6*d*. He also held 2 messuages with their virgates and had an annual lease of 10 a. 3r. 20 p. of demesne arable.[19] This was exceptional, but in 1462 John Dalby held three messuages and virgates, and Alice Bagnale, William Langton, John Bowes and Margaret Callis all held more than two messuages with their virgates, yet there was still vacant land.[20] The declining economy is also evidenced by a reduction in the size of the common oven in 1440.[21]

The medieval field system can be largely reconstructed from later records, including the inclosure award. In 1669, Stonehill field, to the east of the north–south through road (Map 8) extended as far north as the road to Leicester near the northern parish boundary,[22] across an area of later pasture with underlying ridge and furrow, and this may have been its original extent.[23] Other ridge and furrow suggests that Trent Field, divided into two sections in 1778, was originally united and included land to the north of the hospital.[24] The eastern and southern parts of what had become an extended Donington Park by 1778 were largely common grazing (documentary evidence suggest the ridge and furrow on this land dates from the 16th century).[25] The inclosures at Wavertoft, in the south of the parish, belonged to Norton Abbey. Other old inclosures were attached to the castle and hospital, and lay behind the houses. It was recorded in 1669 that the 'Antient Grange House' at Wavertoft had rights of common for ten cows and one bull in Stonehill Field as far as Leicester Way after harvest, and 80 sheep when that field was fallow.[26]

1483–1780

Edward IV extended his park through an agreement of 1483, by exchanging demesne land totalling *c*.500 a. for an unknown quantity of the tenants' common pasture, and possibly other land.[27] This may have necessitated some rearrangement of the open fields, and the laying down of new pasture to the north of the castle.

By 1516, through a combination of the earlier acquisition of vacant holdings and the redistribution of former demesne land, 13 people farmed two-thirds of the land in the parish. Robert Haselrigge, appointed Duchy steward the following year, held nine messuages, three burgages, a cottage, more than seven yardlands of arable and seven parcels of meadow. Other major landholders included widow Agnes Bentley who held

18   Melb. Hall Est. Office, X94/40/2, m. 2.
19   Hilton, *Econ. Development*, 159–61, from TNA, DL 29/183/2903, DL 29/183/2918.
20   TNA, DL 43/6/3; Farnham, 56–63.
21   TNA, DL 29/184/2918.
22   Town bk.
23   R.F. Hartley, *The Medieval Earthworks of North-West Leicestershire* (Leicester, 1984), 52, 55 and pers. comm.
24   Ibid.
25   Below, 52.
26   Town bk, for example, 1669, 1674, 1675, 1678.
27   TNA, DL 42/19, ff. 118-118v; DL 43/6/5, f. 3v.

over 5½ yardlands and William Ironmonger, Thomas Dalby and Nicholas Loow who each held 3 yardlands or more; nine other tenants each held between 2 and 3 yardlands.[28]

The main crops between 1550 and 1600 were barley and peas, both traditionally spring sown, with little wheat, oats or rye grown.[29] Most farmers had twice as much barley as peas in value and volume, and almost all had pigs, chickens and ducks. Grazing rights on common pasture for other livestock were restricted by stint, but by the mid 17th century, and perhaps much earlier, these 'pastures', originally attached to land and cottages, were freely traded.[30] Median numbers of livestock in late 16th-century probate inventories were 14 cattle (including oxen), 8 horses and 15 sheep, with flock sizes between none and 75 sheep. On most farms, the livestock were valued at slightly more than the crops, although there were exceptions. As there were two fulling mills in the parish from at least 1514,[31] the modest numbers of sheep are perhaps surprising, although the low-lying meadow may have been too wet, and the mills may have obtained most of their business from the local monastic estates, or from Derbyshire parishes. After the dissolution, Duchy steward Thomas Grey (d. 1565) acquired Langley priory,[32] and probably kept sheep there, but also allegedly grazed 200 sheep in Donington Park.[33]

There was little change in farming by the 17th century, other than an increase in the number of sheep (median 54 in 20 inventories),[34] but four inventories between 1660 and 1700 include 14 or more horses, suggesting commercial breeding, perhaps for the thriving horse market in Derby.[35] Tax of £30 10s. paid on horses in 1788 was the seventh highest sum paid in Leicestershire.[36]

Following a serious outbreak of cattle disease in 1667, residents agreed to reduce the stint by one-third for three years from 1668,[37] so only 40 sheep could be grazed for each yardland between October and February, and 10 beasts or horses between May and November,[38] with three pastures attaching to cottages.[39] That suggests there may have been as many as 2,400 sheep within the parish, although there is no evidence of such numbers. The population doubled between 1563 and 1670, and more land was put to the plough, with the number of yardlands increased from 60 to 63½ by 1672.[40]

---

28 TNA, DL 43/6/4.
29 This section is based on ROLLR, W+I/1552/46 (Mee); PR/I/5/146 (Pym); W+I/1584/69B (Bailye); PR/I/12/44 (Robey); PR/I/15/136 (Smalley); PR/I/15/130 (Oker); PR/I/1/106 (Campion).
30 Town bk, 1669.
31 TNA, DL 28/26/1.
32 Nichols, III, 862–3.
33 TNA, DL 30/80/1100, mm. 1, 4.
34 ROLLR, PR/I/64/75 (Foxe, 1660); PR/I/71/104 (Gatly, 1670); PR/I/70/218 (Hackstall, 1670); PR/I/73/147 (Bonsall, 1672); PR/I/74/131 (Bucknall, 1673); PR/I/74/173 (Robey, 1674); PR/I/77/153 (Fox , 1675); PR/I/77/138 (Baly, 1675); PR/I/77/124 (Bucknall, 1675); PR/I/79/26 (Twells, 1677); PR/I/79/73 (Wallis, 1677); PR/I/84/184 (Bucknall, 1682); PR/I/85/113 (Getley, 1683); PR/I/89/4 (Bonsall, 1686); PR/I/90/67 (Iremounger, 1687); PR/I/90/41 (Matchett, 1687); PR/I/91/122 (Sutton, 1688); PR/I/101/82 (Mather, 1696); PR/I/104/155 (Kilbourne, 1700); PR/I/106/140 (Nicklenson, 1700).
35 ROLLR, 14D 32/386.
36 H.T. Graf, 'Leicestershire small towns and pre-industrial urbanisation', Trans. LAHS, 68 (1994), 114, citing TNA, E 182/538, part 1.
37 Town bk, 1667, 1668, 1669.
38 Ibid., 1672.
39 Ibid., 1669.
40 Ibid., 1672.

'Sheep pastures' were permanently reduced by half, and other grazing rights by one-third in 1674.[41] A further reduction in the stint was agreed in 1736, by half for sheep and a quarter for cattle, but with four dissentients among 130 residents with grazing rights, an Act of Parliament was obtained in 1738 to confirm this.[42]

The land at Derby Hills was 'stony' and 'barren', and although Donington copyholders had unstinted rights to graze livestock there, few did because of the distance.[43] Wishing to inclose the land without conflict, Sir John Coke and his successors offered to enfranchise the tenants' lands in Donington from 1640 in exchange for them quitclaiming their grazing rights on Derby Hills, the Castle Yard and Ferry Yard.[44] By 1752, three-quarters of the c.200 copyholders had taken up the offer, and all except one of the remainder were converted to rack rents.[45] The Derby Hills land was inclosed in 1770. The 51 tenants who had retained their rights there shared a little over 30 a., with a median award of 1 r. 28 p.[46]

From 1780

Several of Lord Melbourne's tenants at Derby Hills had invested in improvements to their inclosed land by 1805, including drainage and new buildings, and some of them were rewarded with more land when leases expired on unimproved farms.[47]

An Act of 1778 and award of 1779 inclosed the open fields, common pasture and meadow within Castle Donington parish. The Act covered 1400 a. of arable (61 per cent), 290 a. of meadow (12.5 per cent) and 610 a. of pasture (26.5 per cent), although the award suggests the amount of pasture quoted within the Act had been understated by c.350 a., and the amount of arable overstated by a similar amount. 'Ancient' inclosures were not affected. The newly inclosed land was re-allocated to 144 owners, but almost half, just over 1,100 a., was apportioned between just six people including three non-resident owners: 494 a. 1 r. 15 p. to impropriator Leonard Fosbrooke of Shardlow Hall (Derb.), including 250 a. 3 r. 28 p. in lieu of tithes; 221 a. 1 r. 10 p. to vicar John Dalby, comprising personal land and his glebe; 101a. 3 r. 37 p. to his nephew, attorney Thomas Dalby, who undertook the petition for inclosure; 144a. 1r. 20p. to Richard Cheslyn of Langley; 98a. 3r. 7p. to Thomas Dalby's sister Ann and her husband Dr. Thomas Kirkland of Ashby; and 92a. 0r. 25p. to Thomas Roby. At the other end of the scale, 116 owners received less than 20 a.[48] Expenses and the loss of land for the tithe allocation weighed most heavily on those with the least land, but the loss of common grazing within the village also hit hard. The median award to the 72 smallest landowners was just 1 a. 3 r. 19 p., insufficient for the mixed farming which had been seen across the parish. The Act was therefore a catalyst for economic change within the parish, as many turned away from the land, becoming small-scale manufacturers or wage labourers.

41   TNA DL 43/6/5; Town bk, 1700; 1674.
42   ROLLR, DG 8/24; *CJ*, xxiii, 56.
43   Melb. Hall Est. Office, X94/58/6/18; TNA, DL 4/98/28.
44   *HMC Cowper II*, 282; Melb. Hall Est. Office X94/37/2/2, 5-7; ROLLR, DG 8/3, 8/4, 8/11.
45   Melb. Hall Est. Office, X94/58/5/26.
46   10 Geo. III, c. 13; Derb. RO, Q/RI 34.
47   Melb. Hall Est. Office, X94/52/9/2.
48   ROLLR, DE 5251/1.

The 581 a. of crops recorded in 1801 seems unnaturally low. It includes 475 a. of cereals, split almost equally between wheat, barley and oats, indicating a change in farming practices. The 1,189 a. of arable recorded in 1867 appears more reliable,[49] and comprised almost half of all the farmland. This proportion declined to 39 per cent by 1877 and just 20 per cent by 1937. The number of sheep declined from 2,117 in 1867 to 838 in 1907, part of a national trend, while cattle increased, although with some significant fluctuations from year to year. Only 15 per cent of farmers owned all their land in 1867, rising to 29 per cent by 1927.[50] The largest farms before the First World War were mixed, with sales particulars for three tenanted farms in 1902 revealing that Simpson's Farm (103 a.) was 20 per cent arable, Home Farm (182 a.) was 30 per cent arable and Coppice Farm (193 a.) was 38 per cent arable.[51]

The War Agricultural Executive Committee ordered the ploughing up of 133 a. in 1941 and a further 339 a. in 1942, mostly for wheat and oats, and further farmland was taken for the airfield. There were 15 farms of more than 75 a. in 1942, all with cereals, cattle and poultry, but only seven of these had sheep. The largest farm was 455 a., owned by J.G. Shields of Donington Hall.[52] The number of farms fell after the Second World War through consolidation and building development, with the predominant forms of farming by 1977 being dairy and beef herds.[53]

Orchards were a noticeable part of Castle Donington's landscape. Many of the 604 trees growing within the township on land occupied by 30 different people in an undated valuation of c.1571–1625 were probably for fruit,[54] perhaps shipped down the Trent. Orchards remained prominent in the closes behind the houses and across Castle Hill in the late 19th and early 20th centuries,[55] with 40–45 a. of orchards and 5 a. of soft fruit grown until the 1950s, when the acreage began to decline No orchards remained in 1977.[56]

Woodland

The discovery of a Neolithic axe head in the park may suggest early deforestation for farming.[57] Woodland of 12 by 8 furlongs remained in 1086, c.670 a.,[58] probably largely in the vicinity of the park, where the names Great and Little Stocking, Ridings and Shortwood were recorded.[59] Timber trees were numerous in 1278, when 1,600 oaks were sold from 'Astwode' (east wood) for £61 9s. 10d.,[60] implying at least one other stretch of woodland. The slightly higher sum of 100 marks was paid in 1329 for timber from

49   TNA, MAF 68/134.
50   TNA, MAF 68/134; 68/533; 68/1103; 68/1673; 68/2243; 68/2813; 68/3356; 68/4205; 68/4575; 68/5536.
51   ROLLR, DE 1177/70.
52   TNA, MAF 32/379/134.
53   TNA, MAF 68/5536.
54   Melb. Hall Est. Office, X94/40/1/6.
55   OS Map 25", Leics. X.1 (1884 edn), (1901 edn), (1921 edn).
56   TNA, MAF 68/3356, 68/4205, 68/5536.
57   Leics. and Rutl. HER, MLE 7282.
58   *Domesday*, 632; O. Rackham, *The History of the Countryside* (2000), 75.
59   ROLLR, DG30/Ma/64/2.
60   Ibid., 77.

the park, to be felled over three years.[61] Some varieties were grown for specific uses: crabtrees for the corn mills, maple for the malt mill and sallow for the park pales,[62] and a description of the park in 1809 mentions oak, ash, elm, lime and beech.[63] There seems to have been little positive woodland management in the 16th century, with wood for park pales and the mills seemingly cut under the Duchy's authority when required.[64] Little may have changed by 1789, when a visitor noted that 'old oaks are wither'd into most decrepid stumps; and there is not an addition of young trees'.[65] Annual timber sales of oak, ash, elm and larch were advertised in the 1850s,[66] but fallen timber in the park in 1893 had 'accumulated for years'.[67] In 1901 the park estate contained 500 a. of woodland, including 'grand old timber' in the deer park.[68] It has been estimated that over 1,200 trees were felled and not replaced between 1886 and 1969.[69]

The Park

No licence to impark survives, but the park was extant by 1229, when Henry III gave 10 does and a buck to John de Lacy.[70] A perimeter ditch of 442 p. (2,431 yd) made in 1278 might signify an early extension.[71] Part of the perimeter hedge had to be replaced in 1322, when 97 p. (533 yd) were carried off and burnt by the king's soldiers in the course of the rebellion of Donington's lord, Thomas, earl of Lancaster.[72] The grazing was valued at 20s. in 1311.

The park's underwood was valued at 6s. 8d. in 1352.[73] It provided fuel, was baited and laid at the base of fish weirs to attract eels,[74] and used to make 'faggots and hurdles' to prevent flooding.[75] An ancient arrangement to supply the hospital with two cart loads of brushwood from the park each week was not honoured by Hugh Despenser (lord of the manor 1322–6), but this was reinstated in 1331.[76]

The earliest documentary evidence for a park keeper is from 1322.[77] The suggestion by Nichols and others that a keeper was recorded in either 1102 or 1156 is erroneous,[78]

61   *Cal. Close*, 1330–3, 212.
62   TNA, DL 44/105; transcript in Farnham, 67-8.
63   W. Pitt, *A General View of the Agriculture of the County of Leicester* (1809), 171.
64   For example, TNA, DL 42/95, ff. 13, 21v–22; DL 42/96, ff. 107–107v, 136.
65   J. Byng (C.B. Andrews, ed.), *The Torrington Diaries*, II (1935), 76.
66   For example, *Derby Merc.*, 14 Mar. 1855.
67   *Leic. Chron. and Leics. Merc.*, 9 Dec. 1893.
68   ROLLR, DE 1177/70.
69   A. Squires, *Donington Park and the Hastings Connection* (Leicester, 1996), 65.
70   *Cal. Close*, 1227–31, 222.
71   Notts. Archives, Foljambe MSS VI.I (i).iii.
72   TNA, SC 6/1146/9 m. 3; Fox, 245.
73   TNA, C 135/118/28; Farnham, 52.
74   Cooper and Ripper, 16; Leics. and Rutl. HER, MLE 9695 and MLE 4434.
75   TNA, C 135/24/30.
76   *Cal. Close*, 1330–3, 104.
77   TNA, SC 6/1146/9 m. 3; Fox, 246.
78   Nichols, III, 770.

as names within the document confirm the date as 1401.[79] A group who broke into the park in 1360 had time to cut the hay as well as steal deer, suggesting the keeper lived elsewhere.[80] A keeper's lodge may have been built shortly afterwards: archaeology has revealed a small enclosure c.300 yd south of the present Hall, with a ditch to prevent the entry of deer, which contained two buildings of 48 ft and 12 ft in length, that were destroyed by fire. Pottery suggests the site was occupied between c.1375 and 1600.[81] A lodge was noted in 1400,[82] and two in 1539.[83]

The park had been overgrazed by 1400: the herbage, which 'used to be worth 70s,' was valued at just 24s. 10d., and hay had to be purchased for the deer (sovagyne).[84] From 1400, the Duchy's stewards grazed their livestock there, paying £5 2s. for the herbage and pannage in 1516 and 1539.[85] Both the local manorial court and the Court of Duchy Chamber heard occasional presentments and suits for poaching. Thomas Parsons was amerced for 3s. 4d. at the manor court in 1526 for being a 'common hunter' and keeping two greyhounds,[86] and in 1538 park-keeper Hugh Haselrigge was accused of allowing people to hunt in the park with longbows, crossbows and a white shaggy-haired greyhound.[87]

Wishing to enlarge the park to include three adjacent pieces of common pasture known as Great and Little Stocking and Shortwood, which ran from the 'great gate' to Warren close, Edward IV appointed William Hastings, Robert Staunton and two other Duchy officials in 1481 to negotiate with the villagers.[88] The great gate was presumably where the footpath from the village entered the park, Warren Close can be identified from an undated (probably late 18th-century) sketch plan of the park, and a document of 1585 reveals that the former 'Shortwood' had become known as 'the Lawnde'.[89] It took two years to reach agreement, with the king granting to the tenants of the manor 'for ever', 261 a. 2r. 0p of arable land, 53a. 3r. 0p. of meadow, 92 a. 2r. 0p. of pasture, further meadow and pasture totalling 79 a. 1 r. 34 p. (sub-total 488 a. 0 r. 34 p.), three other parcels of meadow of unknown size and Castle Orchard.[90] The amount of land taken into the park in exchange was not recorded.

Map 9 superimposes boundaries of closes shown on early plans onto a map of 1885,[91] and also includes the location of the lodges and possible forge identified by archaeology.[92] The central area may be the park's extent in 1480, and measures c.300 a. All the marked closes, with the exception of Ridings and those to the west of Little Starkey, would have

79   BL, Harleian MSS 568.
80   *Cal. Pat.*, 1358–61, 421.
81   P. Liddle, 'A late medieval enclosure in Donington Park', *Trans. LAHS*, 53 (1977–8), 8–29.
82   TNA, DL 29/728/11987; Farnham, 54.
83   TNA, DL 3/31/G1.
84   TNA, DL 29/728/11987; Farnham, 54.
85   TNA, DL 43/6/4; ROLLR, 7D 53/1.
86   Melb. Hall Est. Office, X94/40/3.
87   TNA, DL 3/32/S1k.
88   TNA, DL 42/19, f. 86v.
89   Huntingdon Libr., HAM 9/14; TNA, DL 44/370.
90   TNA, DL 42/19, ff. 118–118v.
91   OS Map 6", Leics. IX.NE (1885 edn); ROLLR, DG 30/Ma/64/2; Huntingdon Libr., HAM 9/14.
92   Liddle, 'A late medieval enclosure', 8–29.

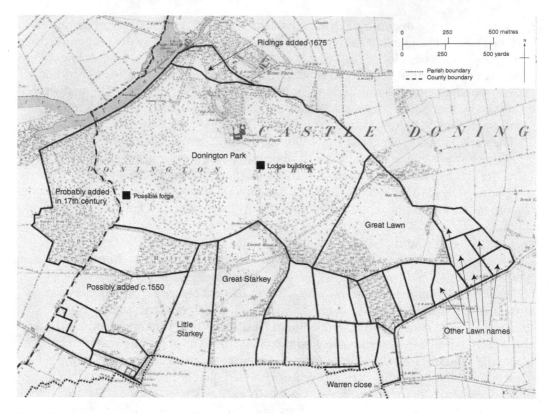

Map 9 *Donington Park, with some of the names recorded on 18th-century plans.*

added a further *c.*400 a., and provides a park boundary of *c.*4.5 miles, against a recorded perimeter of 4 miles in 1529.[93]

The Duchy granted keepership of the park to steward Robert Haselrigge and his son Hugh in 1526,[94] and to Robert's successor Thomas Grey in 1535.[95] Grey complained that Hugh had encouraged tenants to claim new rights of pannage, had allowed cattle to feed in the 'lawnde', and was responsible for a drastic decline in the number and health of the deer.[96] Grey divided the park and launde into seven sections (probably the seven lawn names noted in 1735), three of which he kept for himself to grow flax and hay, probably by rotation, accounting for some ridge and furrow (Map 8). He grazed livestock in the park, including at various times 23 horses, 260 cattle, 240 sheep and 480 pigs.[97] Grey was accused in 1554 of having extended the park by taking the villagers' common 'lee' ground, which provided shelter for cattle in winter.[98] This may have been the land immediately west of Little Starkey sloping down towards Ramsley brook.

93   Melb. Hall Est. Office, X94/52/1/2.
94   TNA, DL 42/22, ff. 92–92v.
95   Ibid., ff. 145–145v.
96   TNA, DL 3/32/S1.
97   TNA, DL 30/80/1100, m 1; DL 3/32/51/S1; DL 3/81/C4.
98   TNA, DL 30/80/1100, m. 4; DL 3/81/C4.

The park was sold by the Duchy in 1595, and became the setting for the 18th-century mansion.[99]

Mines and Quarries

There are gravel pits in the north-east of the parish. The sandstone ridge on the west side of Bondgate was quarried, and there were former stone quarries at King's Mills.[100] John Dalby, Nicholas Joyce and 'Iremonger' held land used for quarrying in 1689.[101] The Duchy provided a licence to the earl of Huntingdon in 1605 to dig for coal at Derby Hills, but with no more than three pits to be open at any one time.[102] By 1633 the lease had expired, with the venture 'of noe use or value'.[103]

Mills and Fisheries

Mills

There was a mill in 1086, valued at 10s. 8d.[104] This may have been in the north-east of the parish, where evidence has been found of an apparent mill dam of the 12th century, with millstone roughouts and baseplates similar to those of an Anglo-Saxon mill house.[105] In the early 14th century, the neighbouring (Hemington) bridge in the north-east of the parish was swept away in a flood,[106] which may also have destroyed this mill. Two watermills, worth £10 in 1311,[107] may have occupied a new site later known as King's Mills. It is almost certain the mills had been moved by 1322, when 'le Flodeyates' is mentioned.[108] This name regularly appears in later records,[109] and suggests a weir had been constructed to control the flow, as does 'Le Waterfal', recorded in 1331.[110] In 1352, the value of the mills was only £5.[111] Repairs cost 25s. 8d. in 1377.[112] By 1400, the mills and mill fishing together were worth £12 14s. 4d., almost one-eighth of the total manorial income.[113] The usual manorial monopoly applied, but the mills were almost two miles

99   Above, 36–9.
100   OS Map 25", Leics. IX.3 (1884 edn).
101   Town bk, Apr.1689.
102   Melb. Hall Est. Office, X94/58/9/1.
103   Melb. Hall Est. Office, X94/40/1/13, f. 2v.
104   *Domesday*, 632.
105   Cooper and Ripper, 39.
106   Ripper and Cooper, 223.
107   TNA, C 134/22/17; Farnham, 49.
108   Fox, 'Ministers' accounts', 243, 269.
109   For example, TNA, DL 29/183/2907, m. 2; DL 28/26/1, f. 1v.
110   *Cal. Close*, 1330–33, 212.
111   TNA, C 135/118/28; Farnham, 52.
112   TNA, DL 29/183/2901.
113   TNA, DL 29/728/11987; Farnham, 54.

from the centre of the village at the foot of a steep hill, so it is unsurprising that twelve men were amerced in 1457 for grinding their corn elsewhere.[114]

Two fulling mills had been added to the two corn mills by 1514.[115] The mill complex was let to steward Robert Haselrigge, and then to his successor Thomas Grey,[116] with an annual rent of £11 6s. 8d. paid in 1539.[117] The corn and fulling mills were 'destroyed' by flooding in 1557, and out of use for 23 weeks. Grey claimed to have spent £121 11s. 4d. on their repair, with £80 refunded by the Duchy.[118] Grey's son was the lessee by Christmas 1581, when another serious flood carried away part of the mills, the weir, the timber and stonework of a large causeway, and 'turned the course' of the river another way; repairs cost £139 6s. 4d.[119] In 1594 the two corn mills stood under one roof 'in the midst of the River', with one fulling mill on the south bank and the other within one bay of building on the north bank. The earl of Huntingdon brought them together under one roof on the south side of the Trent in 1611.[120]

The mill was also accessible to parishes across the Trent, and employed a boatman by 1633.[121] Thomas Smith, a shearman (cloth finisher), leased the fulling mills from the earl in 1633 for £5 quarterly, with a house and a piece of ground for setting tenters for drying new woollen cloth.[122] The lease was renewed in 1644, with an agreement that the earl would repair the damage caused when the property was captured for parliament.[123] The corn and fulling mills, with the associated fishing, were let to William Martin, a cloth worker, in 1674, at £90 for one year.[124]

There was still a working fulling mill in 1683,[125] but a lease had been granted to John Hoffe, a papermaker, in 1680,[126] and the second fulling mill may have been converted for making paper. In 1689, Humphrey Hopkins was assessed for tax of 5s. for 'the paper milnes', the plural suggesting these had now replaced both fulling mills.[127] Machinery for grinding flint is recorded in 1828,[128] but may already have been there some time, grinding flint for the production of Derby porcelain. By 1835, the paper mills were being driven by 'lately erected' steam machinery.[129] A decade later the flint mill on the south bank was grinding gypsum for plaster.[130] The mills were at their post-medieval peak in the mid 19th century, and the terrace of workers' cottages (Map 10) remains in 2016, although converted to hotel accommodation. The corn mills appear to have closed in the

114 TNA, DL 30/80/1090; Farnham, 55.
115 TNA, DL 28/26/1.
116 TNA, DL 1/107/G6.
117 ROLLR, 7D 53/1.
118 TNA, DL 42/96, ff. 184v.–185.
119 TNA, DL 44/335.
120 TNA, DL 44/898
121 Huntington Libr., HAL 11/4.
122 Huntington Libr., HAF 15/31, f. 3.
123 HL, HAF 15/31, f. 1.
124 Melb. Hall Est. Office, X94/58/8/9.
125 Melb. Hall Est. Office, X94/58/8/2.
126 Huntington Libr., HAD 635.
127 Town bk, Oct. 1689.
128 *Pigot's Dir. Leics. and Rutl.* (1828), 476.
129 *Pigot's Dir. Leics. and Rutl.* (1835), 115.
130 W. White, *Dir. Leics. and Rutl.* (Sheffield, 1846), 337.

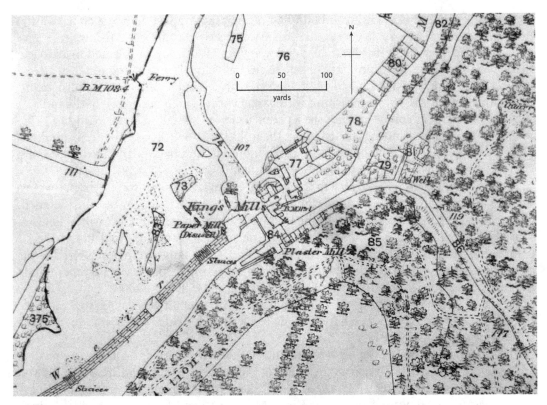

Map 10 *King's Mills in 1882, with workers' cottages (south of the approach road).*

late 1850s,[131] the paper mills towards the centre of the river (Map 10) closed in 1875,[132] and the plaster mills continued until the early 20th century.[133] Substantial remains of the water wheels survived serious fires in 1927 and 1980.[134]

A tower windmill was built in the south of the parish in *c*.1773, atypically turned by a tailpole and winch. The sails were replaced by an engine in *c*.1926.[135] It was demolished when the land was purchased for the airfield in 1942.

Fisheries

Archaeology has revealed a series of fish weirs in the north-east of the parish in a paleochannel of the Trent, comprising three V-shaped lines of wooden posts with wattle fences, one to capture young eels swimming upstream and two to capture mature eels migrating seawards. Radio-carbon dating reveals the first is from the 7th or 8th century, the second from the 9th or 10th century and the final weir from the 11th or 12th century. There is also evidence of fishing from a stone weir of the early 12th century. The fish

131 *PO Dir. Leics. and Rutl.* (1855), 25; W. White, *Dir. Leics.* and Rutl. (Sheffield, 1863), 483.

132 *Derby Merc.*, 27 Oct. 1875; OS 25", Leics. IX.3 (1882 edn).

133 On OS Map 25", Leics. IX.3 (1903 edn), but 'disused' by 1921 edn.

134 *Derby Daily Telegraph*, 27 May 1927; Squires, *Donington Park*, 15.

135 N. Moon, *Windmills of Leicestershire and Rutland* (Wymondham, 1981), 96.

were caught in weighted brushwood bundles, or in basket traps, two of which have also been found. A late Bronze Age structure in the same area may also be a fish weir.[136]

The entire river along the boundary, between both banks, was confirmed in 1310 to belong to the manor of Donington,[137] and the annual value of the fishing was 13s. 4d. in 1311.[138] By 1322 the fishing had been divided, with 14s. 2d. coming from the farm of net fishing, and £1 2s. 4d. from fishing with baskets or traps (corbellorum) at the mill.[139] Further sub-division followed, with six separate fisheries named in an account of 1377, let for £2 14s. 10d., excluding the fishing at the mills.[140] Stone-filled timber cribs found at Hemington quarry created eddies to attract salmonoids, and have been dated to the 14th century, a period when fish weirs had been banned.[141]

In 1511, the Duchy let the ferry to the prior of Beauvale (Notts.) for 40 years, together with a [fish]weir and certain fishing rights in the river,[142] which appear to have included all the fishing except that attached to the mills. This was replaced in 1532 with a new 80-year lease, at 61s. for the ferry and 'Ferrie Man meadow', and 50s. for the fishing.[143] The prior sub-let the fishing for 10s. plus half of the fish,[144] and assigned the unexpired term of the head lease to Christopher Eyre in 1538. After passing through several other hands, the residual term was assigned to Sir George Hastings in 1589 for £200.[145] It formed part of the assets of the manor bought by the Cokes in 1633, when it was valued together with the ferry at £5 11s.[146] By 1808, Charles Crane of Cavendish Bridge had lost money on the fishing for several years.[147]

The fishing attached to the lease of the mills was known as 'mylne pitt' or 'mylne depe' and may not have extended across the width of the river. The mills and their fishing were valued at £5 in 1326, and £12 14s. 4d. in 1400.[148] Two sturgeon, one 7½ ft long and the other measuring 9 ft, were caught near King's Mills on 10 and 12 August 1644.[149] A single haul taken between Cavendish Bridge and Donington Hall in 1821 netted 99 salmon,[150] but later industrialisation and pollution reduced fish stocks.

In 1901, fishing rights upriver for 2.5 miles from Kings Mills were included within the sale of the Hall, with rent of £70 payable to earl Cowper, lord of the manor, for part of this stretch. Sub-leases to Thomas Wood, Wellington Angling Society and Midland Railway Fishing Club returned £125 annually.[151]

136 Leics. and Rutl. HER, MLE 4463.
137 Tait (ed.), *Cart. Chester*, II, 475–7.
138 TNA, C 134/22/17; Farnham, 49.
139 TNA, SC 6/1146/9, m. 3; Fox, 242, 268.
140 TNA, DL 29/183/2901, rot. 2.
141 Cooper and Ripper, 8.
142 TNA, DL 42/95, ff. 21v–22.
143 Derb. RO, D779/T/108.
144 TNA, DL 3/34/G2c.
145 Derb. RO, D779/T/108; TNA DL 1/95/T12.
146 Melb. Hall Est. Office, X94/57/6/4.
147 Melb. Hall Est. Office, X94/52/9/2.
148 TNA, DL 29/728/11987.
149 *HMC Hastings I*, 392.
150 *Derby Daily Telegraph*, 27 Feb. 1907.
151 ROLLR, DE 1177/70, pp. 3, 16.

Manufacturing

Introduction

There is little evidence of manufacturing in the medieval period, although the 1379 poll tax includes the names Couper, Glover, Spynner, Taylour, Smyt, Barker and Webster.[152] Although most probate inventories of the 16th and 17th century, including two thirds of those taken between 1675 and 1699, include agricultural assets,[153] some farmers also had by-employments. John Bucknall (d. 1675) possessed three stones of wool and woollen yarn, and may have been a merchant as well as a farmer.[154] Henry Bailye (d. 1584) had a substantial farm, but also had fleeces and wool (in November), dressed hemp, a spinning wheel and three different types of new cloth.[155] Simon Fox (d. 1581) and Thomas Roby (d. 1674) had substantial farms. Fox also had 50 yd. of new cloth, and Roby had 32 yd. of new and 40 yd. of hurden cloth.[156]

Inclosure changed the occupational structure of what had been 'merely an agricultural village' in 1779.[157] In 1801, 247 of the 390 people whose occupations were recorded in the census were chiefly employed in manufacture, trade or handicrafts.[158] Most of this was small-scale production, but a few larger workshops and factories developed, including a three-storey lace factory by 1839.[159] The collapse of the lace and knitting industries by the 1850s caused hardship and migration, although the trades did not disappear: there were 328 people employed in the lace industry in Castle Donington in 1851, 221 employed in hosiery, glove-making or embroidery, and 54 basketry workers.[160] The opening of two factories in 1863 and 1870 might have seemed to herald better times, but there were only four major employers in 1910: one hosiery factory, one lace factory, a blouse factory and the brewery at Cavendish Bridge.[161] These industries had all but disappeared by the mid 20th century, but manufacturing had revived by 2015 across a wide range of sectors, from automotive engineering to clothes and furniture.

Basket-making

Donington's traditional industry was basket-making, using osiers which grew alongside the Trent, and the baskets used to catch eels in the medieval fish weirs were probably made locally.[162] Land with osiers at Milneholme was let with one of the fisheries for 12s.

---

152 *Poll Taxes 1377–81* (ed.) Fenwick, I, 547–8.

153 Graf, 'Leicestershire', 109.

154 ROLLR, PR/I/77/124.

155 ROLLR, W+I/1584/69B.

156 ROLLR, PR/I/74/173.

157 *Poor Law Commission*, App. 383C.

158 Census enumeration (1801), 179.

159 *Derby Merc.*, 6 Nov. 1839.

160 Census 1851.

161 ROLLR, DE 2072/95.

162 As found, for example, at Hemington quarry: L. Cooper and S. Ripper, 'Castle Donington, Hemington quarry, western extension', *Trans. LAHS*, 75 (2001), 137–42.

in 1377.[163] In 1554, Robert Roby grew osiers on land alongside the Trent which he and his ancestors had enjoyed for many years.[164] On his death in 1605, Andrew Walton, a scuttle-maker, held an unexpired lease of osier beds valued at 11s., osiers of 'sundry sorts' worth 32s. 6d. and sallows and ash woods worth 10s.[165] In 1675 Donington's inhabitants agreed to inclose five parcels of common grazing by the river and let these for 10 years, on condition that the land was planted with osiers 'in such manor [sic] as may be most advantageous to the Towne', with the rents applied for the benefit of the inhabitants. The leases were renewed for a further ten years in 1685 and again in 1695.[166]

By the 19th century, basket-making was mentioned as one of the main occupations in every trade directory, and children and infants were regularly kept off school for up to two months in the spring to peel osier rods.[167] It was an adaptable trade, with products including lunch hampers and chairs. Despite a trade depression in the mid 1890s,[168] 72 heads of households were employed as basket-makers in the 1901 census – more than any other occupation.[169] The industry enjoyed its last period of prosperity during the First World War, making shell baskets for artillery (Fig. 9). Although primarily a male occupation, wives and daughters stitched the leather bands on the shell baskets. The industry was one of two main employments in 1936 (the other being hosiery),[170] but it was declining. By 1948, there were few craftsmen left, and the osier beds were described as 'derelict'.[171]

Knitwear and Lace

Thomas Glover (d. 1729) was a framesmith,[172] suggesting there may already have been several stocking frames in the village. By 1801, there were two framework knitting workshops on the upper floors of houses by the Turk's Head.[173] In 1833, Donington had 'the character of a manufacturing town', with full employment, including work for women and children seaming hosiery and figuring lace,[174] with three silk hosiery manufacturers, five lace-makers and three framesmiths recorded in 1835.[175] There were 97 frames in employment in Donington in 1844, 46 of which were used to make gloves, with the remainder making fully fashioned hosiery, mostly in cotton or silk.[176]

Two separate sections of the lace industry were present in Donington: bobbin net and warp blonde. The bobbin net trade expanded rapidly across the East Midlands,

163 TNA, DL 29/183/2901, m. 1.
164 TNA, DL 30/80/1100.
165 ROLLR, PR/I/1606/21/51.
166 Town bk, 1675, 1685, 1695.
167 ROLLR, DE 5569/1, pp. 200, 206-10, DE 5569/2, pp. 202, 211.
168 *Second report from Selection Committee on distress from want of employment*, Parl. Paper (1895 (253), viii), p. 113.
169 Census 1901.
170 *Kelly's Dir. of Leics & Rutl.* (1936), 56.
171 *Derby Daily Telegraph*, 15 Sept. 1948.
172 ROLLR, PR/I/119/117.
173 *Leic. Jnl*, 13 Feb. 1801.
174 *Poor Law Commission* (Parl. Papers, 1834 (44) xxvii), app, p. 280A, 280C.
175 *Pigot's Dir. Leics. and Rutl.* (1835), 116.
176 *Framework Knitters Com.*, part II (Parl. Papers, 1845 (641), xv), appendix, pp. 4–5.

Figure 9 *Castle Donington's basket workers made baskets for artillery shells in the First World War*

but overproduction led to a collapse in prices in the late 1820s.[177] Five bobbin net manufacturers with six machines in Castle Donington joined an initiative in 1829 to restrict hours to preserve the trade, but with 15 bobbin net machines in the village in 1831, not every manufacturer took part.[178] Nottingham lace-makers employed 'several hundred females' in Castle Donington to embroider lace in 1835,[179] and the collapse of the trade affected many families, with 1835–6 the worst year.[180] It took time to recover, but in 1864 a girl aged 10 or 12 could earn 3*s*. weekly by making trimmings or braid.[181] This work continued into the early 20th century, with many women 'chevoning' (embroidering hose) for Leicester firms.[182]

Simon Orgill patented an application of the Dawson wheel for lace-making in 1807.[183] He had a three-storey workshop on Mount Pleasant, and also established a partnership with William Follows, who had a lace workshop on Borough Street.[184] On the night of

177 W. Felkin, *A History of the Machine-wrought Hosiery and Lace Manufactures* (1867), 332–5.
178 S.A. Mason, *Nottingham Lace, 1760s–1950s* (Ilkeston, 1994), 83, 206.
179 *Pigot's Dir. Leics. and Rutl.* (1835), 115.
180 Felkin, *A History*, 351.
181 ROLLR, DE 5569/2, p. 30.
182 1901 census enumerator's bk; J. Carswell (ed.), *My Castle Donington: Memories of Castle Donington before 1950* (Coalville, 1991), 15.
183 Mason, *Nottingham Lace*, 29, 76, 322; *The Repertory*, 10 (1807), 318–19; *Framework Knitters Com.* (Parl. Papers, 1845 [609], xv), p. 23.
184 Mason, *Nottingham Lace*, 322; ROLLR PR/T/1817/147.

10–11 April 1814,[185] a mob entered Orgill's premises and 11 of his 12 warp lace frames were 'reduced to a heap of ruins'.[186] He was awarded £400 damages at Leicester Assizes, to be paid by West Goscote Hundred,[187] but on appeal, the judges of the King's Bench were unanimous that lace frames were not covered by the statutory protection, so no damages should be paid.[188] Orgill's business was taken over before 1828 by Jonathan Woodward and Company. There were at least another 14 lace-makers in Donington in the early 19th century, and the village was badly affected when 'warp blonde' went out of fashion in the 1850s.[189]

An old factory was reopened in 1863 by hosiery manufacturers Wells and Co. of Nottingham.[190] A silk mill of 18 bays and two storeys was built on Station Road in 1870 by Watson and Co. of Beeston (Notts.). It employed 200 people,[191] including children who attended school on three days in one week and two the next, alongside their factory work.[192] The Castle Donington New Industries Co. built a factory in Victoria Street in 1895 which was let to Nottingham hosiery manufacturers, Gibsons,[193] the main employer in Donington in the 1920s and 1930s.[194] Watson & Co. became bankrupt in 1902,[195] but after renovation the silk mill still presented an impressive facade in 2015 as rented office accommodation.

Ironworking

Indications of metal working have been found within the park (Map 9).[196] The Duchy granted miller Christopher Croft a 21-year lease and licence in 1592 at 30s. annually to build an iron forge above the corn and fulling mills.[197] Within six months, the inhabitants had complained that it was diverting too much water from the mill, and depriving them of their common.[198] The annual rent of 30s. was paid in 1617 by the earl of Huntingdon,[199] but it is possible that no ironmaster was employed. By 1640, the forge was 'decayed and quite downe'.[200] A new lease was granted in 1654 to Thomas Woolshouse to build another on the same land,[201] but this may not have been built. A forge or iron

185 *The Times*, 10 Nov. 1815, p. 3.
186 *Morning Chron.*, 21 Apr.1814, p. 2.
187 *Bury & Norwich Post, or, Suffolk, Norfolk, Essex, Cambridge and Ely Advertiser*, 16 Apr. 1815.
188 *The Times*, 10 Nov.1815, p. 3; 3 May 1817, p. 3.
189 Mason, *Nottingham Lace*, 322–3, 5, 95.
190 *Derby Telegraph*, 2 May 1863.
191 W. White, *Dir. Leics. and Rutl.* (Sheffield, 1877), p. 182; *Leic. Jnl*, 22 Apr. 1870.
192 ROLLR, DE 5569/1, pp. 201 –2; DE 5569/2, pp. 205–6.
193 Signature bk Nottm. Joint Stock Bank (formerly held at Midland Bank, Castle Donington; whereabouts unknown in 2016).
194 Taylor, *Dwelling in the Past*, 2.
195 *Nottingham Evening Post*, 22 Oct. 1902.
196 Liddle, 'A late medieval enclosure', 28.
197 TNA, DL 42/98, f. 222–222v; DL 42/47, ff. 202v–203.
198 TNA, DL 42/98, f. 225; DL 4/36/4.
199 TNA, DL 43/6/5.
200 TNA, DL 4/98/28.
201 Huntington Libr., HAD 627.

smithy within the manor at Derby Hills was described as 'newly built' in 1628,[202] but of 'noe use or value' by 1633.[203]

Brewing and Malting

A horse mill for grinding malt was built near the village green shortly before 1490.[204] By custom it had a monopoly, but in 1537 one burgage holding included a malt-kiln, in 1551 the vicar was using malt querns at home,[205] and by 1574 several residents had their own malt querns.[206] John Coxon had a kiln and malt house in 1625,[207] John Bucknall had a 'milnehouse' in 1634, and John Webster was amerced in 1680 and 1682 for grinding malt for copyholders.[208]

A brewery and malthouse were built at Cavendish Bridge in 1815 by John Fletcher and Sons. The business was purchased by George Eaton before 1841,[209] whose executors sold it in 1896 to Offilers Brewery of Derby.[210] By then, the brewery buildings included a two-storey, 17-bay maltings.[211] In 1901, the brewing and malting industry employed 36 heads of households in Donington.[212] Offilers centralised their operations in Derby in 1923,[213] but in 2014 a micro-brewery was among a number of small businesses trading on the site.

Tannery

A newly-built brick house with tanyard was advertised for sale in 1764,[214] and again in 1774.[215] This may have been on Bondgate, where there was a tannery in 1846.[216] By 1872, this included two covered bark sheds with a capacity of 300 tons, heated drying sheds, two steam engines and pumps.[217] It had closed by 1901.[218]

Engineering and Modern Manufacturing

Norton Motorcycles (under new ownership) moved to Donington Park in 2008, where a factory was established to develop a new model which could be tested on the adjacent

202 Melb. Hall Est. Office, X94/58/5/26.
203 Melb. Hall Est. Office, X94/40/1/13, f. 2v.
204 TNA, DL 30/80/1091, m. 2.
205 J. Laughton, 'Castle Donington' (unpubl. MS), 5; Melb. Hall Est. Office, X94/40/3, m. 2.
206 TNA, DL 1/86/G4, 1/107/G6, 1/124/A35, 1/128/A43, 1/132/A38.
207 ROLLR, PR/I/31/120.
208 Town bk, 1680, 1682.
209 Pigot & Co., *Dir. Leics. and Rutl.* (1835), 116; (1841), 8.
210 Ex. inf. Mr. E.C. Offiler, Former Managing Director, Offiler's Brewery, Derby.
211 M. Palmer (ed.), *Leicestershire Archaeology: The Present State of Knowledge,* III (Leicester, 1983), 15.
212 Census, 1901.
213 *Derby Daily Telegraph*, 18 Dec. 1922.
214 *Derby Merc.*, 9 Mar.1764.
215 Ibid., 2 Sept. 1774.
216 W. White, *Dir. Leics. and Rutl.* (Sheffield, 1846), 337, 340.
217 *Derby Merc.*, 6 Nov. 1872.
218 OS Map 25", Leics. X.1 (1901 edn).

race track.[219] The business moved their headquarters to Donington Hall in 2013, with production and a training academy in Hastings House, an adjacent modern building.[220]

A number of manufacturers had units on the two commercial parks at Trent Lane and Willow Farm in 2014, making components for the car and aircraft industries, digital machines for textile companies, lighting, kitchen cabinets and stationery.

Retail

John Roby was described as a wool buyer in 1395,[221] and Richard Hyrnemonger sold nails and keys to Grace Dieu Priory between 1414 and 1418,[222] his surname suggesting his ancestors may have been selling iron goods for several generations. By the 17th century, a number of Donington's farmers had large stocks of bacon and cheese at their deaths and may have been traders, including Hugh Iremoner (d. 1675), who had 37 cheeses at his death, but only three cows.[223]

Markets and Fair

In 1278, Henry de Lacy was granted a weekly market on Wednesdays, and an annual fair of three days, on the vigil, day and morrow of St Edward.[224] The market had the potential to take trade away from the established Thursday markets at Derby and Loughborough, and may have traded before 1278. A memorandum of May 1279 notes payment of 3s. 7d. for the expenses of the merchants in the castle on St Edward's day, for the 'improvement' of the fairs,[225] suggesting the weekly market had been moved to the castle when the usual location was required for the fair's stalls. The church dedication was to St Edward King and Martyr in 1490, but in the year to May 1279 none of his feasts would have clashed with a Wednesday market. A fair held around either of the feasts of St Edward King and Confessor, on 12–14 October 1278 or 4–6 January 1279, would have begun on a Wednesday, and this record may point to the original dedication of the church.[226]

With five other markets within eight miles, Donington's market appears to have struggled to survive in the longer term.[227] A new Tuesday market was established at Kegworth in 1290,[228] and while Donington's market was valued at 30s. in 1311, perhaps

219 http://www.nortonmotorcycles.com/company/history/ (accessed 1 Jul. 2014).

220 http://www.nortonmotorcycles.com/company/donington-hall.html (accessed 1 Jul. 2014); http://www.leicestermercury.co.uk/Norton-teams-Halfords-tilt-TT/story-21164732-detail/story.html; http://www.leicestermercury.co.uk/Youngsters-set-rev-skills/story-21346595-detail/story.html (accessed 1 Jul. 2014).

221 *Cal. Pat.* 1391–6, 630.

222 D. Johnson (ed.), *Grace Dieu Priory Leicestershire: the Draft Account Book of the Treasuresses, 1414–1418* (Ashby-de-la-Zouch, 2013), 47, 85, 123, 151.

223 ROLLR, PR/I/77/157.

224 *Cal. Chart.* 1257–1300, 207.

225 Notts. Archives, DDFJ 6/1/1.

226 TNA, DL 30/80/1091, m. 2.

227 S. Letters, *Gazetteer of Markets & Fairs in England and Wales to 1516*, http://www.history.ac.uk/cmh/gaz/gazweb2.html (accessed 14 Aug. 2013).

228 *Cal. Chart.* 1257–1300, 346.

including the fair, neither market nor fair were mentioned in a valuation of 1352.[229] Those baking and selling bread between 1457 and 1482 were residents,[230] but in 1490 the bakehouse was *devastat*,[231] and by 1510, external bakers dominated, many from Nottingham or Loughborough. Donington's butchers, who had supplied the local market before 1513, were also displaced by butchers from elsewhere, including Kegworth and Aston-on-Trent.[232] In 1617, the residents gave evidence that there was neither market nor fair.[233]

A market was held twice weekly in 1814, on Wednesdays for corn and on Saturdays for other goods,[234] and the 'first revived fair' for horses and livestock was held that year.[235] By 1846, only a weekly Saturday market was held, with annual fairs on 18 March (the feast of St Edward, King and Martyr), Whit Thursday and Michaelmas, as well as a statute fair in late October for hiring servants.[236] The fairs had ceased by the 1870s,[237] with the exception of the statute fair, which was reduced to a single day, and continued until at least 1905, when hiring was 'not brisk'.[238] By 1881 the market had been discontinued, although livestock were still sold on alternate Mondays from a paddock near the railway station.[239] A monthly farmers' market was held in 2015. There was also a large 'car supermarket' in 2015, occupying *c*.9 ha. on Station Road.

Shops

The earliest clear evidence of a shop is from the inventory of chandler Michael Pymme (d. 1681). As well as his 'candle house' with tallow and equipment, he had a 'shop' with stocks of ribbon, lace, buttons, caps, tobacco and pipes.[240] Other shops presumably also existed, but only 12*s*. 4½*d*. was collected in shop tax in 1785, compared with £3 18*s*. 3*d*. in Loughborough.[241] By then there was at least one large store, run by Messrs Erpe and Richdale until 1791, selling many different fabrics and haberdashery items, gloves, stockings, hats, tea and coffee.[242] Trade directories from the 19th century show a wide range of shops in Borough Street, Clapgun Street and Bondgate, selling almost everything anyone could need. Borough Street remained the main shopping street in 2015, with most of the shops family-owned. Most employment was then on the fringes of the parish, with many people using the supermarket near the industrial estate, or shopping outside the parish.

---

229 TNA, C 135/118/28; Farnham, 52
230 D. Postles, 'An English small town in the later middle ages: Loughborough', *Urban History*, 20 (1993), 28–9, based on TNA, DL 30/80/1090–1101.
231 TNA, DL 30/80/1091, m. 2.
232 Postles, 'An English small town', 28–9.
233 TNA, DL 43/6/5.
234 *Nottingham Gaz.* 11 Feb. 1814.
235 *Derby Merc.*, 3 Mar. 1814, 3.
236 W. White, *Dir. Leics. and Rutl.* (Sheffield, 1846), 337.
237 Ibid. (Sheffield, 1863), 483; (Sheffield, 1877), 182.
238 *Derby Daily Telegraph*, 2 Nov. 1905.
239 C.N. Wright, *Dir. Leics. and Rutl.* (Leicester, 1887–8), 374.
240 ROLLR, PR/I/83/88.
241 TNA, E182/537 part 2.
242 *Derby Merc.*, 14 Jul. 1791.

Services

Banks

It is notable that no early banks were seen in Donington,[243] although a Penny Bank to encourage saving among the poor was organised from 1858 and continued until at least 1862,[244] when a branch of the Post Office Savings Bank had opened.[245] By 1879, there was sufficient business for the Nottingham Joint Stock Bank to open a branch on Borough Street, which moved to larger premises in Market Place in 1900. In 1905 it became the London City and Midland Bank through amalgamation,[246] later becoming Midland Bank, and then HSBC. It remained open as a branch of HSBC in 2015.

Warehouses and distribution

By 1642, Leonard Fosbrooke had three or four boats each of 10–12 tons burden at Wilden Ferry, and was shipping lead and other commodities downriver to Nottingham. Sir John Coke agreed that year to assist with arrangements to transport arms required by the army in Ireland up the Trent from Nottingham to King's Mills, as part of their journey from Hull to Chester.[247]

Between 1711 and 1762 the Fosbrooke family had the only warehouses on the Trent between Nottingham and Burton.[248] In 1710, Leonard Fosbrooke made an agreement with the cheesemongers of the city of London to carry all cheese delivered to Wilden Ferry downriver to Gainsborough, for shipment to London.[249] Warehouses at Cavendish Bridge were raided during the food riots of 1766, and over three tons of cheese were stolen.[250] Following the opening of the Trent and Mersey canal in 1770, river trade was diverted to Shardlow, which became an inland port.[251] It created local employment: 70 heads of household earned their living as boatmen in the 1841 census, offsetting the impact of the depression in the lace and knitwear industries.[252]

Warehousing and distribution formed a major part of Donington's economy in 2015: several logistics and distribution companies were based at Willow Farm Business Park, and in 2014, international carrier DHL moved its headquarters and main UK hub to Donington,[253] on premises attached to the airport, near the Royal Mail hub. Delivery companies UPS and TNT Express also had depots at the airport in 2015. In the north-

---

243 M. Dawes and C.N. Ward-Perkins, *Country Banks of England and Wales, Private Provincial Banks and Bankers, 1688–1953* (2000).
244 *Derb. Chron.*, 2 Oct. 1858. *Derby Telegraph*, 27 Sept. 1862.
245 W. White, *Dir. Leics. and Rutl.* (Sheffield, 1863), 486.
246 Ex. inf. J. Mortlock, archivist, HSBC.
247 *HMC, Cowper II*, 306.
248 Above, 6.
249 Melb Hall Est. Office, X94/57/1/14.
250 *Leic. and Nottingham Jnl*, 11 Oct. 1766.
251 *Derby Merc.*, 11 May 1770.
252 Census enumerator's bk.
253 http://www.leicestermercury.co.uk/DHL-invest-90m-East-Midlands-hub/story-21309480-detail/story. html.

west of the parish, a new distribution depot for Marks and Spencer opened in 2012 on the site of the former power station. The 900,000 sq.ft warehouse was claimed to be the largest e-commerce depot in Europe, handling up to one million items each day and employing 1,200 workers during seasonal peaks.[254] The Secretary of State for Transport granted planning permission in 2016 for a major rail-freight interchange to be built on 250 a. (101 ha.) of land in the adjoining parish of Lockington-cum-Hemington, to be served by a spur from the line through Castle Donington. It was projected to create a further 7,000 jobs in the locality.[255]

Hotels

Donington was little more than a village in 1686 when a survey of guest beds and stables recorded five guest beds and stabling for five horses.[256] Although two turnpike roads passed through the parish by 1760,[257] Donington was not an overnight stop, but was a convenient place to pause. Tax of £52 12s. was paid on wagons and coaches in 1788, the third highest figure in the county.[258] Three large inns stood near the village green by the end of the 18th century: the Rawdon, in older premises which were substantially rebuilt in 1794 to include stabling for 11 horses,[259] the Turk's Head, described as a 'new brick house' in 1801,[260] and the Moira Arms. The former Turk's Head and Moira Arms were no longer hotels in 2015. The Rawdon had closed by 1850,[261] but reopened as Donington Manor Hotel in 1967,[262] and in 2015 was the only hotel in the centre of the village. There was also a hotel in 2015 at King's Mills, several bed and breakfast options across the parish and two camping and caravanning parks near Donington Park. The Donington Arms, near the station, traded as a hotel in the early 20th century,[263] but lost much of its trade when the station closed.

The opening of the airport and growth of its passenger business, coupled with good road links to many parts of the country, drove demand for hotel accommodation and conference facilities on a larger scale, to suit different pockets. In 2015 there were four large hotels on Pegasus Business Park, adjacent to the airport.

Professional Services

Two generations of the Dalby family were solicitors in Donington in the late 18th and early 19th centuries. By 1835, there were four attorneys in the village,[264] and although

---

254 http://www.leicestermercury.co.uk/pound-82-5m-deal-sell-ex-M-amp-S-warehouse-Castle/story-20335494-detail/story.html; http://allportcargoservices.com/retailnews/allport-knowledge/archives/mon/5/yr/2013/1 (accessed 1 Jul. 2014).

255 http://www.bbc.co.uk/news/uk-england-leicestershire-35301865 (accessed 28 Feb. 2016).

256 TNA, WO 30/48.

257 11 Geo. II c. 33; 33 Geo. II c. 41.

258 E 182/538 part 1, cited in Graf, 'Leicestershire', 114.

259 Lee, 'The rise and fall', 57; Leics and Rutl. HER, MLE 11450; Ryder (1997), 55–6.

260 *Leic. Jnl*, 13 February 1801.

261 Lee, 'The rise and fall', 57.

262 NW Leics. District Council, *Castle Donington Conservation Area Appraisal and Study* (2001), 7.

263 ROLLR, DE 2072/95, p. 32.

264 *Pigot's Dir. Leics. and Rutl.* (1835), 115.

that number fell, over the remainder of the 19th and 20th centuries there has always been at least one lawyer in Donington. In addition to solicitors and accountants based in the village, two major accountancy firms opened large offices on Pegasus Business Park in the 21st century: PwC (PricewaterhouseCoopers) with 300 employees in 2013,[265] and PKF Cooper Parry in 2014, with 200 employees.[266]

Three companies offered serviced office space in 2015: at Pegasus Business Park, in the old vicarage on the market place, and in the former silk mill on Station Road.[267]

Motor Racing

Donington Park has played a prominent role in motor sport at the national and international level since 1931, when John Gillies Shields engaged Fred Craner to create a racing circuit of 2 miles 327 yd. in the south-east of the park,[268] the second British racing circuit, after Brooklands (Surrey).[269] In 1933, permission was given for cars with engines up to 3 litres to use the track,[270] and Donington was chosen to host Britain's first Grand Prix in 1935.[271] The circuit was improved and enlarged in 1937, and at just over 3 miles, was the longest and fastest in Britain,[272] attracting German teams in 1937 and 1938, and numerous spectators.[273] Racing ceased in 1939,[274] plans to resume racing shortly after the army left in 1956 fell through,[275] and go-kart racing in 1962 led to complaints about noise.[276] The racetrack was sold in 1971 to businessman and motor enthusiast F.B. (Tom) Wheatcroft, whose collection of Grand Prix cars opened there as a visitor attraction in 1973.[277] Objections to resuming racing were overcome in 1976,[278] and a rebuilt circuit of 1.957 miles opened in 1977.[279] An additional loop added in 1985 increased the circuit to 2.5 miles, enabling it to host the British Motorcycle Grand Prix from 1987 to 2010 and the European Grand Prix (Formula 1) in 1993, but attempts from 1988 to stage the British Grand Prix finally failed in 2009.[280]

265 http://www.derbytelegraph.co.uk/PwC-celebrates-10-years-Castle-Donington/story-18481689-detail/story.html (accessed 31 Dec. 2015).
266 http://www.leicestermercury.co.uk/Accountancy-firm-s-new-office-bright-bold-bit/story-21150965-detail/story.html (accessed 1 Jul. 2014).
267 http://www.novaloca.com/office-space/to-let/castle-donington/ (accessed 30 Jan. 2016).
268 *Derby Daily Telegraph*, 24 Apr. 1931; Leics and Rutl. HER, MLE 16249.
269 *The Times*, 29 Mar. 1938.
270 *Derby Daily Telegraph*, 18 Aug. 1933.
271 Ibid., 5 Oct. 1935.
272 *The Times*, 29 Mar. 1938.
273 A short film of the 1938 Grand Prix is available at https://www.youtube.com/watch?v=TZT1GOqY9kI accessed 21 Mar. 2016.
274 *The Times*, 4 Oct. 1937; 19 Aug. 1955; 29 Aug.1939.
275 Ibid, 16 Oct. 1957; 10 Jul.1962.
276 Ibid., 12 Feb. 1963.
277 http://www.donington-park.co.uk/about-donington/tom-wheatcroft/ (accessed 24 Sept. 2014).
278 *The Times*, 16 Jan. 1976.
279 Ibid., 13 Nov. 1976.
280 *Autosport*, 1 Nov. 2009.

Festivals

In 1980, Donington Park staged Monsters of Rock, a single-day rock festival which returned almost every year until 1996. After a break with only the occasional festival, the first Download rock festival was held in 2003, initially over two days. By 2016, this had become an established annual event, consistently attracting over 100,000 people to an extended three-day programme.[281]

Utilities

A gas company was formed in Castle Donington in 1853, and a gas works built for £2,000 at Spittal, funded by the issue of shares.[282] Unfortunately the gas failed at the celebratory dinner arranged to mark the completion of the project.[283] The company was taken over by the Draycott Gas Company in 1907,[284] which was in turn taken over by Long Eaton Gas Co. in 1922.[285] The brewery at Cavendish Bridge and the Hall had their own gas supplies.[286] The change to natural gas resulted in the closure of the gas works in the 1970s.[287]

Mains water was supplied from 1892 by the Long Eaton (Derbs.) local board,[288] replacing the many pumps across the village. Water was pumped from boreholes at Stanton-by-Bridge to a reservoir in Castle Donington, east of Hill Top,[289] which was delivered to houses by gravity feed. A second reservoir within the parish opened in 1930.

The first electricity was supplied by the Leicestershire and Warwickshire Electric Power Company.[290] In 1950, the British Electricity Authority announced that they would build a power station at Castle Donington, to employ 1,500 people.[291] The 190 a. site was in the north of the parish, adjacent to the river and railway line. With six units each generating 100,000 kilowatts, it was the largest power station in Europe when it opened in 1958, burning 7,100 tons of coal each day.[292] A high-speed rail delivery system was introduced in 1981.[293] Following closure in 1994, the site was assessed by English Heritage as being of 'national importance', due to its size,[294] but with no statutory protection, it was demolished in 1996.[295] Two major electricity supply companies, National Grid and Western Power, were based in large offices at Pegasus Business Park in 2015.

281 https://downloadfestival.co.uk/experience/history/.
282 *Derby Merc.*, 6 Jul. 1853.
283 *Notts. Guardian*, 1 Dec. 1853.
284 *Derby Daily Telegraph*, 20 Nov. 1907.
285 ROLLR, QS 75/23.
286 Ex inf. British Waterways (1950s); Leics. RO, D533/A/TC/40, 223–4; *Derb. Chron.*, 10 Aug. 1867.
287 NW Leic. District Council, *Castle Donington, Conservation Area Appraisal and Study* (2001), 30.
288 *Kelly's Dir. Leics. and Rutl.* (1895), 49.
289 OS Map 25", Leics. IX.8 (1902 edn).
290 *Kelly's Dir. Leics. and Rutl.* (1936), 55.
291 *Derby Daily Telegraph*, 8 Mar. 1950; 1 Jun. 1950.
292 Central Electricity Generating Board, *Castle Donington Power Station* [Official opening pamphlet, 1958], 9–10 (copy in Derb. Local Studies Libr.).
293 *The Times*, 12 Aug. 1981.
294 Leics and Rutl. HER MLE 4462; Estell Warren, 'Castle Donington Power Station Site, Regional Storage and Distribution Centre, Archaeological Desk Top Assessment' (Unpubl., 1999), 7–8 (copy at Leics County Hall).
295 https://www.facebook.com/bbc.emt/videos/1314618875221866/ (accessed 29 Apr. 2016).

SOCIAL HISTORY

Social Structure

CASTLE DONINGTON WAS ALWAYS a minor estate of lords whose main estates were elsewhere, and whose personal interests were in national politics.[1] Yet the creation of a deer park by 1229, and its extension in 1483, suggests they visited at least occasionally, and they played a major role in the development of Donington as a medieval town, building the castle and hospital, and obtaining a charter for a market and fair. Attempts at urban development resulted in a mixed economy of burgage holders, farmers and cottagers, but without a dominant local figure. Resident stewards and secular landowners from the 16th century altered the balance of local society, but the rise of religious nonconformity in particular, suggests that aristocratic influence remained weak. Following the rise and gradual collapse of manufacturing industry in the parish in the first half of the 19th century, Castle Donington once again assumed a rural aspect, and its self-declared status as a village was generally accepted in the early years of the 21st century.

The Middle Ages to *c.*1600

The recorded population in 1086 was mostly unfree, comprising a priest, five sokemen, 30 villans and 11 bordars,[2] similar proportions to those seen locally in Tonge, Worthington and Melbourne.[3] The establishment of the market, creation of burgage tenure, and the absence of a resident lord, aided by urban development, may have encouraged inward migration. Burgesses are mentioned from 1311,[4] and 43 burgage plots, held by customary tenure, were listed in 1462.[5] There were just five freeholders in 1331, probably the successors of the sokemen of 1086, whose land was apparently less profitable than trade. Only three of them were assessed for tax in 1327, at 12*d.*, 15*d.*, and 2*s.* respectively, well below the mean assessment of 2*s.* 9*d.*[6] In 1332, the two largest tax assessments were 8*s.* 10¼*d.* for Matilda atte Barre and 6*s.* 8*d.* for Humphrey le Draper,[7] both names suggestive of urban life. Early 14th century tax assessments do not list values

1   Above, 28–31; *Complete Peerage*, vii, 681–6, 154–9.
2   *Domesday*, 632, 648.
3   Ibid., 636, 742, 752. Lockington and Hemington were not recorded, although there would almost certainly have been settlements there.
4   TNA, C 134/22/17.
5   TNA, DL 43/6/3.
6   TNA, E 179/133/1, rot. 12.
7   TNA, E179/133/2 rot 1d.

of lands or goods, so we cannot tell whether Donington was taxed at the urban or rural rate, but there was a wide disparity between rich and poor. With just 27 taxpayers that year, but 280 residents over the age of 14 enumerated in the 1377 poll tax,[8] it appears that most people were living at subsistence level.

A detailed rental of 1462 reveals a complex social structure, presumably established before the Black Death, with inhabitants classified as freeholders, burgesses who performed no works, burgesses who owed works, customary tenants (mostly holding one messuage and virgate), 'acremen' who performed no works (renting a small amount of land, too small to support a family), 'acremen' who owed works, and cottagers. Empty plots and reduced rents had enabled some to acquire second and third holdings, while others rented half or quarter burgages. Two families who became prominent long-term landholders had emerged: William Rooby was a freeholder, having bought William de Saxton's land, and John Dalby rented three messuages with three virgates of land.[9] Rooby was probably a descendant of John Roby of Castle Donington, a wool-buyer in 1395.[10] An exchange of land with the Duchy in 1483 to facilitate the expansion of the park enabled some to increase their landholdings, and by 1516, just 13 people farmed two-thirds of the land in the parish, although this was still copyhold.[11] Only Thomas Roby and Robert Osbourne were assessed for tax on land in 1524, paying 3s. and 2s. respectively, while 27 men paid tax on goods, with a mean assessment of 3s. 1d., and eight others paid tax of 4d. on their wages.[12] With 70 households in 1563,[13] around half of all families were too poor to be taxed.

The stewards and constables appointed by the duchy of Lancaster from 1400 were initially men of standing and wealth, who exercised their responsibilities through deputies. This changed after the execution of steward William, Lord Hastings, in 1483. Robert Staunton (steward from 1485), Robert Haselrigge (from 1517) and Thomas Grey (from c.1538) were resident, and may have exercised social leadership. Grey appears to have assumed the mantle of an overbearing lord. The many complaints against him included overgrazing common land with sheep, and compelling tenants to provide horses and carts when he marched against the accession of Queen Mary.[14] His illegitimate son Thomas inherited his lease over Donington's mill,[15] and possibly his arrogance, but received no Duchy office and was afforded little respect. John Robye commented that he would not cease to bring law suits against Grey 'whilst they two lived'.[16]

Social Structure from c.1600

Edward Hastings and Francis Beaumont held a lease of the manor from 1591 to 1610, and in 1595 Edward's brother George bought the Park. The arrival of one of the

8   *Poll Taxes 1377–81*, (ed.) Fenwick, I, 484–91.
9   TNA, DL 43/6/3; Farnham 56–63.
10   *Cal. Pat.*, 1391–96, 630.
11   TNA, DL 43/6/4.
12   TNA, E179/123/324, pt 1, rot. 3.
13   A. Dyer and D.M. Palliser (eds), *The Diocesan Population Returns for 1563 and 1603* (Oxford, 2005), 224.
14   TNA, 30/80/1100, m. 6; DL 3/81/C4.
15   TNA, PROB 11/48/274; DL 42/22, ff. 300v–302.
16   TNA, DL 44/370.

county's foremost political families as principal landowners provided opportunities for aristocratic patronage, employment and trade, and their residence supported the growth of a small professional class in the village. They may also have introduced tensions within the community during the Civil War. Henry Hastings, the 5th earl's son, was appointed colonel-general of the king's Midlands army in 1643,[17] while the younger Sir John Coke (lord of the manor) supported Parliament.[18]

The hearth tax of 1664 exposes the gulf between the living standards of the villagers and those at the Park, and also reveals a small middling class: 92 residents had one or two hearths, 22 people were taxed on three, four or five hearths,[19] while above them stood Thomas Roby, with 11 hearths, and the dowager Countess of Huntingdon (the 7th earl being a minor) with a total of 40 hearths.[20] Roby had acquired land and property in Donington which had been forfeited by Thomas Coke MP for deserting parliament,[21] and in 1669 held one messuage, five yardlands, three cottages and a double burgage.[22] The Dalby family gained prominence: John Dalby headed the middling group of taxpayers in 1664, with five hearths,[23] and had become a freeholder by 1669 by purchasing Henry Osbourne's house and land.[24]

The enfranchisement of 150 of the c.200 copyholders between 1650 and 1752[25] changed the social structure of the village, and evidences weak landowner control, as does occasional civil unrest and the widespread adoption of nonconformist beliefs. Distrust of middlemen grew nationally when corn prices rose in 1766, and a 'mob' of c.100 people broke into a warehouse at Cavendish Bridge, stealing one ton of cheese. When the owners of the cheese entered the village to request search warrants from a Donington magistrate, he refused to assist, perhaps fearing retaliation. Residents hurled brickbats and stones at the cheese owners and their party, chasing them to Cavendish Bridge, where a further two tons of cheese was stolen from the warehouse, and cheese worth £900 was taken from a boat moored downriver. Donington's church bells rang in celebration, suggesting the churchwardens' sympathies were with the people, and a hogshead of beer was distributed.[26]

There is little evidence of the social relationship between the Hastings family and the village in the 17th and 18th centuries. The religious fervour of Countess Selina,[27] widowed in 1746, led to the formation of many new congregations in local villages and further afield, but had little impact in Donington itself, although the reason is unclear. It may relate to the relationship between the Hastings and Coke families, whose lands perfectly mirrored each other: the Hastings owned Donington Park and the

17   *ODNB*, s.v. 'Hastings, Henry, Baron Loughborough' (accessed 24 Nov. 2015).
18   *ODNB*, s.v. 'Coke, Sir John, (1563–1644), politician' (accessed 26 Jan. 2015).
19   TNA, E 179/251/4.
20   TNA, E 179/251/4.
21   *Cal. Cttee for Compounding*, III, 1844, 1848.
22   Town bk.
23   TNA, E 179/251/4.
24   Town bk.
25   Melb. Hall Est. Office., X94/37/2/2, 5-7, X94/58/5/25, X94/58/5/26; ROLLR, DG 8/3, DG 8/4, DG 8/11.
26   *Leic. and Nottingham Jnl*, 11 Oct. 1766.
27   Below, 101.

neighbouring manor of Melbourne from 1605,[28] while the Cokes owned Melbourne Hall, and the manor of Castle Donington.

Inclosure created a class of landowner with small, uneconomic, plots and some large compact estates. Leonard Fosbrooke received a substantial inclosure allotment of 220 a. 3 r. 28 p. in lieu of the great tithes, alongside his existing landholding of a similar amount, giving him a similar acreage within the parish to the earl, although Fosbrooke's land was divided and sold by 1831. Inclosure also cemented the position of the Dalbys. Vicar John Dalby was allotted 139 a. 1 r. 14 p. of land in his own right, in addition to his glebe holding, while his nephew Thomas Dalby, an attorney, received 101a. 3 r. 37 p.[29] Thomas's two sons, Thomas, a lawyer, and John, vicar from 1807,[30] enjoyed a close professional relationship with Lord Rawdon, the three of them meeting at very short notice in 1817 to discuss a claim to the Huntingdon earldom by a distant cousin of the 10th earl.[31] The Dalby family continued to be major landowners in the 20th century.[32]

Civil disobedience appeared more threatening in 1792, given developments in France, and men of property were keen to encourage loyalty to the crown. Led by an anonymous 'party of gentlemen' who fired volleys, Donington became the first of several Leicestershire towns and villages to stage a mock trial and the burning in effigy of the radical, Tom Paine, and again, the church bells were rung.[33] By the end of that year the Kegworth and Castle Donington Association for Promoting the King's Proclamation to Defend the Constitution Against all Innovations had been formed. Resolutions were passed to subscribe, buy and circulate 'proper books', and prevent the spread of seditious writings and words,[34] and a prosecution was brought against Donington clockmaker Robert Erpe for saying on two occasions that he thought there would be no king by March.[35]

Residential areas were mixed, with the occupants of High Street in 1841 including lawyers, farmers, people of independent means, and also labourers and shop-workers.[36] The number of factories and workshops grew after inclosure,[37] but these were mostly small and located in residential streets. The most prominent industrialist was George Eaton from Sutton (Derb.), who had purchased the Cavendish Bridge brewery by 1841,[38] and built workers' houses and a school for the children of his employees,[39] effectively creating a new residential settlement within the parish. His daughter, Miss Juliana Eaton, became a foundation manager of the parochial school in 1908,[40] and served on both parish and district councils in the 1920s.[41]

---

28   ROLLR, DE362/S/Temp1, p. 8.
29   ROLLR, DE 5251/1.
30   Lincs. Archives, Reg. XL (Act bk).
31   H.N. Bell, *The Huntingdon Peerage* (1820), 230–1.
32   *Kelly's Dir. Leics. and Rutl.* (1912), 55; (1932), 58; (1941), 55.
33   *Leic. Jnl*, 9 Nov. 1792.
34   *Leic. Jnl*, 21 Dec. 1792.
35   TNA, TS 11/1073/5143.
36   Census enumerators' bks.
37   *Poor Law Commission*, Parl. Papers (1834, (44) xxvii), App., p. 381C, 384C.
38   Pigot & Co., *Dir. Leics. and Rutl.* (1835), 116; (1841), 8.
39   *Derb. Chron.*, 15 Oct. 1859; *Derby Merc.*, 24 Oct. 1860.
40   *Loughborough Monitor*, 25 Jun. 1908.
41   *Derby Daily Telegraph*, 24 Feb. 1928; ROLLR, DE 1524/96.

Figure 10 *A folk dance festival at Donington Hall in 1931.*

By the 19th century, a close paternalistic and philanthropic relationship had developed between Hall and village: local children attended steeple-chasing in the park,[42] the Hastings family occasionally visited the school and requested half-day holidays,[43] and a small library of books was presented by the dowager marchioness in the 1830s and kept at the vicarage.[44] Christmas and New Year balls in Donington Hall were given regularly for tenants and tradesmen,[45] and the 4th marquis distributed 120 large pieces of beef to families in the winter of 1864–5.[46] Military bands played in Donington Park on Sundays, although this entertainment was not universally popular and 292 inhabitants petitioned parliament in 1856 for this to cease.[47]

Times were more straitened after the death of the 4th marquis in 1868, although the countess and Lord Donington continued the tradition of providing coal to poor residents at Christmas from the family collieries.[48] A relationship was maintained after the sale of the park in 1903, for example with Major Gretton hosting a coronation tea in 1911.[49] Festivals in the Park in the 1930s attracted local people as well as visitors (Fig. 10). Gillies Shields (d. 1943) was closely involved in parish life, serving as a councillor at parish,

42   ROLLR, DE 5569/2, pp. 10–11.
43   For example, ROLLR, DE 5569/1, p. 26.
44   ROLLR, 1850'245/50/1, p. 85.
45   *Derby Telegraph*, every Christmas 1850–67.
46   Ibid., 18 Jan. 1865.
47   *Military Bands on Sundays* (Parl. Papers 1856 (281), lii), p. 4.
48   *Derby Merc.*, 11 Dec. 1861; *Leic. Chron.*, 30 Dec. 1871; *Derby Daily Telegraph*, 29 Dec. 1887.
49   CADMT, 2010.17.37.

district and county levels,[50] and presided at military tribunals hearing appeals against conscription in the First World War.[51]

The social hierarchy had all but disappeared by the Second World War.[52] Post-war residential and commercial development changed the character of Castle Donington yet further, from a small dormitory village with little employment, but a strong sense of community, where 'everyone knew everyone else', to a large settlement, with substantial employment on the fringes of the parish, attracting commuters who lived, and often shopped, elsewhere.

Community Activities

Sports

A team from Castle Donington met a team from Aston-on-Trent for 'footeball play' in Aston (Derb.) in June 1624. It was a violent clash, resulting in the death of a man and causing the Earl of Huntingdon, as Lord Lieutenant of the county, to cancel the inter-county game arranged for the following day between Long Whatton (Leics.) and Barton (Notts.).[53] A modern football club was formed in 1885,[54] and in 2015 its teams played at Spittal Park. A rugby union club, formed in 1987, also played at Spittal Park in 2015.[55] A team from Castle Donington lost a cricket match against Derby in 1792,[56] but there is no evidence of regular matches then. Schoolmaster Richard Willson helped to establish the sport in Donington for boys from 1858,[57] and adults in 1861.[58] The team has not enjoyed a continuous existence, but matches have been played in most decades. In 2014 the first team played in the Derbyshire Premier and County Cricket League, with home matches played at Moira Dale recreation ground.[59]

A tennis club was formed in 1926, playing on land off Delven Lane rented from Miss Juliana Eaton. The land was given to the parish after her death, and the courts continued to be used until the 1970s. There was a bowls club at Park Lane by at least 1852,[60] and the game was played there until 1940. A new green opened in 2004 on the former tennis courts,[61] and a new club pavilion opened in 2015.[62] A Petanque club started at the Nag's Head c.1980 as a result of Castle Donington's twinning with Gasny (department Eure) in Normandy, and in 2014 had a membership of c.20.[63] A nine-hole golf course was laid

---

50   ROLLR, DE 500/150/9; *Derby Daily Telegraph*, 19 Apr. 1929, 21 Aug. 1936, 12 May 1943.

51   *Derby Daily Telegraph*, 6 Mar. 1916.

52   F.B. Harvey, *Archibald W. Harrison: An Appreciation* (1945), 4–5.

53   *HMC, Hastings, IV* (1947), 206–7.

54   CADMT, 2004.5.745

55   http://www.pitchero.com/clubs/castledoningtonrufc/ (accessed 1 Jul. 2014).

56   *Derby Merc.*, 20 Sept. 1792; 27 Sept. 1792.

57   *Leics. Merc.*, 28 Aug.1858.

58   *Derby Merc.*, 18 Sept. 1861.

59   http://castledonington.play-cricket.com (accessed 1 Jul. 2014).

60   *Notts. Guardian*, 6 May 1852.

61   http://www.cdbowlsclub.co.uk/clubhistory.html (accessed 1 Jul. 2014).

62   http://www.nwleics.gov.uk/pages/castle_donington_bowls_club_pavilion/ (accessed 30 Dec. 2015).

63   http://www.thursday-petanque.org.uk/viewclub.php (accessed 1 Jul. 2014).

out in Donington Park in 1935,[64] and a club was formed under the presidency of J.G. Shields,[65] but was forced to close when the army requisitioned the Hall and Park in 1940, and did not reopen.

Donington was hunted by the Quorn, but the 2nd marquis bought a pack of hounds in 1833,[66] and 'borrowed' the area,[67] with meets held at various locations including Cavendish Bridge.[68] Following his death in 1844, the hounds were supported by subscription and hunted by Sir Seymour Blane and John Story.[69] The pack was sold following the death of the third marquis in 1851,[70] and the area 'accepted back' into the Quorn.[71] Shooting parties were held at the Park. At one 'grande battue' in December 1829, over 300 head of game were killed in three and a half hours;[72] three days' shooting in the home covers in 1866 netted 3,486 head.[73] Flat racing and steeple chases took place at the Park in the 1860s.[74]

Other Community Activities

A brass band was formed in 1864, and engaged regularly for friendly society anniversaries, events at the Park and other occasions.[75] The annual hiring fair, known as the 'Wakes', was held in late October, and included stalls, roundabouts, shooting galleries and, in 1841, hyenas and a leopard.[76] The Wakes survived in 2015 as a three-day funfair, with stalls on the village streets.

The Castle Donington Mutual Improvement Society was 'in a flourishing condition' in 1852, with its own library.[77] Lectures were held on topics as diverse as the history of printing, the human body, and John Bunyan.[78] Penny readings and musical events raised money to help poorer residents.[79] Occasional entertainments included visits by Joseph Smedley's theatre in 1812,[80] and 'Wilton's troupe of Christy's Minstrels' in 1869.[81] Political meetings were held by Castle Donington Conservative Association, formed in 1886,[82] and by the Liberals in the early 20th century.[83] Victoria Hall, formerly the Independent

64   *Derby Daily Telegraph*, 1 Jun. 1935.
65   Ibid., 16 Dec.1935.
66   Leic. *Chron.*, 23 Nov. 1833.
67   C.D.B. Ellis, *Leicestershire and the Quorn Hunt* (Leicester, 1951), 134.
68   *Derby Merc.*, 12 Mar. 1851.
69   *Derby Merc.*, 10 Apr. 1844.
70   *Derby Merc.*, 2 Apr. 1851.
71   Ellis, *Leicestershire*, 79, 134.
72   *Derby Merc.*, 23 Dec. 1829.
73   *Leic. Jnl*, 7 Dec. 1866.
74   Ibid., 18 Dec. 1863, 7 Dec. 1866; *The Field*, 19 Dec. 1863.
75   For example, *Derby Merc.*, 25 May 1864; 28 Jul. 1869; 27 Nov. 1889; 23 May 1894.
76   *Leics Merc.*, 30 Oct. 1841; *Derby Merc.*, 3 Nov. 1869.
77   *Notts. Guardian*, 29 Jan. 1852.
78   *Derby Merc.*, 5 Dec. 1860; 3 Nov. 1869; 8 Dec. 1869; *Notts. Guardian*, 28 Feb. 1861.
79   *Notts. Guardian*, 26 Apr.1867; *Derby Merc.*, 17 Mar. 1869.
80   Lincs. Archives, LHS 35/5/1/2.
81   *Derby Merc.*, 8 Dec. 1869.
82   Ibid., 24 Feb. 1886.
83   *Nottingham Evening Post*, 29 Nov. 1904.

chapel, was used from 1897 by a 'Pleasant Sunday Afternoon' organisation.[84] The building later became a Sailors' and Soldiers' Club. A Floral and Horticultural Society held large annual exhibitions in the 1850s and 1860s with prizes for flowers, fruit, vegetables and cottage gardens,[85] and continued into the 20th century.[86]

A branch of the British Legion was formed in 1921, the year the village war memorial was unveiled on High Street.[87] Castle Donington Women's Institute began in 1929, with a monthly programme of activities, demonstrations, talks and competitions, and continued to meet in 2014.[88] A Rotary Club was formed in 1974, and had 31 members in 2014,[89] and a Probus club for retired professional and business people began to meet in 1980 and had 50 members in 2014.[90] Other long-standing clubs included an antiques circle, meeting from the 1960s until 2012,[91] and a local history society, founded in the 1970s and active in 2014.[92] The Boy Scouts celebrated their centenary in 2013,[93] when it was the largest group in the Loughborough District, with 110 Beavers, Cubs and Scouts, and 21 adult leaders. Girl Guides and Army Cadets have also met in the town for many years. Castle Donington Museum Trust began life in the 1970s as a committee of the parish council, became a charitable trust in 1994 and in 2015 was an accredited volunteer-run museum.[94]

Social Welfare

Castle Donington had three friendly societies in 1803, with a total membership of 240.[95] The 'Old Monday' sick club had been founded in 1784, and had 300 members by 1849. A Female Benevolent Society was formed in 1799, and in 1849 there was also a lodge of Oddfellows.[96] Moira Lodge, affiliated to the Imperial Union, had been founded in 1828,[97] but appears to have been short-lived. Another lodge named after the Earl of Moira, but affiliated to Manchester Unity, was formed in 1843.[98] Five societies were noted in 1863: Loyal Hastings Lodge, Female Hastings Lodge, Loyal Moira Lodge, the Old Monday's

84 *Derby Daily Telegraph* 14 Apr. 1897.
85 *Derby Merc.*, 7 Aug. 1861; 12 Apr. 1865.
86 *Kelly's Dir. Leics. and Rutl.* (1904), 53.
87 *Derby Daily Telegraph*, 13 Jan. 1921.
88 http://www.aboutmyarea.co.uk/Derbyshire/Derby/DE74/News/Whats-On/237649-Castle-Donington-Womens-Institute-Programme-2013 (accessed 1 Jul. 2014).
89 http://www.aboutmyarea.co.uk/Derbyshire/Derby/DE74/Community/Clubs-and-Organisations/34366-The-Rotary-Club-of-Castle-Donington (accessed 1 Jul. 2014).
90 Ex inf. Probus club member.
91 Ex inf. former member.
92 Ex. inf. Bruce Townsend, founder and group leader.
93 http://www.cdscoutgroup.co.uk (accessed 1 Jul. 2014).
94 http://www.castledoningtonmuseum.org/about/ (accessed 1 Jul. 2014).
95 *Returns on the Expense and Maintenance of the Poor* (Parl. Papers 1803–4 (175), xiii), 259–60.
96 *Derby Merc.*, 6 Jun. 1849.
97 *Leic. Jnl.* 11 Jul. 1828.
98 *Friendly Societies* (Parl. Papers 1880 (365), lxviii), 338–9; *Nottingham Review and General Advertiser*, 22 Sept. 1843.

Club and the Old Wednesday's Female Lodge.[99] By 1900, there was also a Wesleyan Women's Sick and Benefit Society, whose membership was said to be growing.[100]

Moira Lodge (Manchester Unity) appears to have been the most successful of the societies. It owned 7 a. of land in Castle Donington in 1845, which was divided into allotments for the benefit of its 180 members,[101] and later purchased land at Hill Top and Mount Pleasant.[102] Following a decision by the directors of Manchester Unity to reduce the level of sickness benefits, 370 members of Moira Lodge voted to secede from the Manchester Order in 1902, believing local funds were strong enough to sustain higher benefits. Two dissentient members transferred to another lodge in the Derby district, while the remainder formed the Castle Donington Independent Friendly Society,[103] which chose to backdate its formation to 1844.[104] It became an 'approved society' in 1911, enabling it to administer the National Insurance scheme: as a result, membership increased to 581 in 1923. It continued to own and let allotments, to 250 people in 1923.[105] In 1972 it sold its land at Mount Pleasant to the parish council for £8,200,[106] and in 1983, the decision was taken to wind up the society, realise remaining assets and distribute this sum to its members.[107]

Poor Relief

Poor Relief to 1834

The earliest surviving record of the administration of poor relief is the appointment of new overseers in 1657.[108] Detailed annual accounts do not survive, but annual totals were frequently recorded in the town book, with occasional schedules of the sums collected from individuals, presumably as a source of reference for future years. In 1682, most poor relief was paid to widows, generally up to 6*d.* weekly in cash together with coal, although in 1683 widow Cooper received coal and 5*s.* to purchase a stone of hemp 'by consent'.[109] The parish was attractive to migrants, but the officers were vigilant and acted swiftly to prevent a legal settlement being gained, for example presenting John Sutton to the manor court in 1676 for providing lodging to a stranger.[110]

Nine boys and five girls were apprenticed by the parish in 1661, apparently within Donington, including four children of widows and one who was probably illegitimate, but this may have been an exceptional year. There is no mention of providing training

99   *Derby Merc.*, 11 Mar. 1863.
100 *Leic. Chron.*, 8 Sept. 1900.
101 *Framework Knitters Com.* (Parl. Papers 1845 [609], xv), p. 126.
102 ROLLR, DE 8371.
103 *Derby Daily Telegraph*, 24 Jan. 1902; ROLLR, DE 8371.
104 *Derby Daily Telegraph*, 16 Jul. 1903.
105 Ibid., 8 Jun. 1923.
106 ROLLR, DE 8371.
107 CADMT, 2011.17.115–116.
108 Town bk.
109 Ibid.
110 Ibid.

in 1688 when basket-maker Henry Hodgkinson agreed to 'take & keepe at my owne cost' Margaret Footit to the age of 21 in return for three annual instalments of 30s., and shepherd John Pim agreed to maintain Mary Footit for three years for a total payment of £2 3s. 4d. The children's mother was still alive, but the agreement was presumably designed to save the parish money. The same year, a house owned by the parish, with a yard and hovel, was let for life to John and Frances Bosworth for 1d. annually 'if it be demanded', together with seven annual loads of coal, in exchange for taking in and maintaining Samuel Iremonger until he was able to provide for himself.[111]

By 1768, there were 27 houses for the poor 'on the common belonging to the freeholders', whose occupiers paid annual rents to the field reeves of between 1s. and 30s.[112] These properties were vested in the churchwardens and overseers under the Inclosure Act of 1778.[113] By 1803 there was also a parish workhouse, where 23 paupers lived, including children.[114] The cost of poor relief increased substantially from £289 in the early 1780s to £1,543 11s. 0d. in 1820,[115] but then reduced during the lace boom of the 1820s which provided employment.[116] Per head of population, the cost was far lower than in most Leicestershire parishes, but the farmers resented paying poor rates based on a 1779 valuation, as the owners of factories and workshops built since inclosure managed to resist revaluation by outvoting the farmers at vestry meetings.[117]

Poor Relief from 1834

Perhaps fearing that the 1834 Poor Law Amendment Act would soon prevent the parish from selling its houses, a vestry meeting was called in that year, when one churchwarden and the two overseers presented a case for selling the cottages and gardens and using the proceeds to build a new infant school.[118] The proposal was accepted, and three of the houses were sold at auction, with eviction notices served on the residents. The properties raised less than their true value, as there were doubts that the parish officers had the power of sale, and there were 'tears & lamentations', as the occupiers could not afford to rent elsewhere, but the Poor Law Commission chose not to become involved.[119]

Shardlow poor law union was formed in 1837, comprising 46 parishes in Derbyshire, Nottinghamshire and Leicestershire, including Castle Donington.[120] Donington was the largest parish, and provided three of the 57 guardians. Shardlow already had a workhouse, which was enlarged in 1838–9. Twenty of Donington's remaining 'town houses' were sold in 1841 to clear the parish's share of the capital cost of this enlargement,[121] but other houses were retained. These included the former parish

111 Town bk.
112 Ibid., 1768.
113 18 Geo. III, c. 20.
114 *Poor Rate Returns* (Parl. Papers 1803–4 (175), xiii), pp. 258–9.
115 *Report of Select Cttee on Poor Rate* (Parl. Papers 1822 (556), v) p. 86.
116 *Poor Rate Returns* (Parl. Papers 1830–31 (83), xi) p. 100; *Poor Law Commission* (Parl. Papers 1834 (44), xxvii), App. B, p. 280A.
117 *Poor Law Commission* (Parl. Papers 1834 (44), xxvii), App., p. 381C, 384C.
118 TNA, MH 12/2060/1835.
119 Ibid.
120 TNA, MH 12/2060/1837.
121 TNA, MH 12/2061/1841.

workhouse in the castle moat, which became a parish meeting room,[122] until partly demolished in 1928 due to 'serious decay'.[123]

The nonconformist churches also played an important role in helping the poor. In exchange for a small weekly sum, women from the Baptist church bought fabric and made clothes for poor children in the 1840s. The Baptists also had a poor relief fund,[124] as did the Wesleyans.[125]

Charities

Castle Donington has had several charities for the benefit of its poor, with 21st-century mergers ensuring the modest income from each could be distributed to best advantage.

Thomas Gray, a 'gentleman' of King's Newton in Melbourne parish (Derb.) left £200 in 1691, with the income to provide grey coats or waistcoats annually to six poor residents of Castle Donington, 15 dozen loaves for Donington's poor, and similar aid for the poor of Melbourne parish, with any surplus to provide apprenticeships for poor children.[126] Seven children from Castle Donington, chosen by the inhabitants at vestry meetings, were apprenticed by this charity between 1830 and 1835.[127] Thomas Twells, a shepherd, bequeathed the income from 1 a. of land in Hemington in 1700 for the benefit of the poor of Castle Donington, and a cash endowment of £5 to provide a small sum each year for distribution among the village's shepherds. The landholding was reduced to just 1 r. 24 p. when Hemington was enclosed in 1789,[128] and the income was absorbed into the overseers' accounts for many years, but began to be distributed again by the vestry from 1833.[129] Income of £5 in 1908 was shared between 40 people.[130] The money for the shepherds could not be traced in 1839.

Little is known about 'Bonsor', who gave land to the annual value of 17s. 2d. to the poor of the parish, and the name of another person who gave land of a similar value had been forgotten by 1839. Another donor whose name had also been forgotten gave land worth 34s. 4d. for the benefit of eight poor widows.[131] At inclosure, a charity known as 'Bonsors and others' was awarded 1 a. 0 r. 35 p. of land,[132] half for the benefit of eight widows and the remainder for the poor more generally.[133] Arthur Eyre left the residue of his estate in 1877 for the benefit of the 'aged and indigent poor inhabitants'. Although the probate value was less than his specific bequests,[134] between £2 and £4 was distributed

122 *Leic. Chron.*, 23 Jul. 1892.
123 *Derb. Advertiser,* 3 Feb. 1928.
124 C. Clayton, *The History of the General Baptist Sunday School Castle Donington* (1890), 28.
125 ROLLR, DE1168, N/M/64/61.
126 *Report of the Charity Commissioners* (Parl. Papers 1826–7 (426), x), p. 296.
127 *Report of the Charity Commissioners* (Parl. Papers 1839 (163), xv), p. 374.
128 Ibid., pp. 374–5; ROLLR, PP 348.
129 *Report of the Charity Commissioners* (Parl. Papers 1839 (163), xv), pp. 374–5.
130 *Kelly's Dir. Leics. and Rutl.* (1908), 55.
131 *Report of the Charity Commissioners* (Parl. Papers 1839 (163), xv), p. 375.
132 ROLLR, DE 5251/1.
133 *Returns of Charitable Donations* (Parl. Papers 1816 (511) xvi), pp. 646–7; *Report of the Charity Commissioners* (Parl. Papers 1839 [163], xv), p. 375.
134 Leicester Probate Registry, 5 Mar. 1878.

annually in the early 20th century.[135] The charities of Thomas Gray, 'Bonsor and others' and Eyre were merged in 2001 through the creation of a new charity, 'Thomas Gray', which works to alleviate poverty and assist groups which contribute to the quality of life.[136] James Farmer, a local pharmacist who died in 1901, left a terrace of ten houses to be used as almshouses for 'poor widows of good character' aged over 60 and resident in Castle Donington for at least five years.[137] Farmer's properties were converted into ten flats in the 1960s, and in 2014 this charity was in the process of being merged with Twells' charity.[138]

Education

Day Schools before 1780

Harold Staunton founded a chantry in 1512, whose priest would also teach grammar, 'for the erudycyon of pore scolers within a scolehouse',[139] making Donington one of just five Leicestershire towns and villages known to have had a permanent school before the Reformation.[140] The duchy of Lancaster agreed to continue the school when the chantry was dissolved,[141] and the chantry priest was still employed on a pension as schoolmaster in 1554.[142] It is not known how long this school continued. Good literacy levels are evidenced by probate inventories and parish accounts of the late 16th and 17th centuries are written in many different hands, but residents may have been taught informally. Only two schoolmasters are known to have taught here in the 17th century: Cockain, ejected for nonconformity in 1662,[143] and John Daniel, who taught in 1676.[144] A bequest of £10 by Elizabeth Bucknall in 1707 for a school was included on a charity board in the church,[145] but the vicar advised there was no school at each visitation from 1706 to 1721.[146] Title deeds identify a school in Borough Street in the 1720s,[147] but its history is not known.

Sunday Schools

A Sunday school was established in the opening years of the 19th century, and run jointly by members of the Wesleyan and Baptist congregations on non-sectarian lines. The

---

135 *Kelly's Dir. Leics. and Rutl.* (1908), 55; (1928), 58.
136 Charity 219155, http://www.charitycommission.gov.uk (accessed 23 Jul. 2013).
137 *The Times*, 20 Dec. 1901.
138 Ex inf. a trustee of Farmer's charity.
139 TNA, PROB 11/17/257.
140 N. Orme, *English Schools in the Middle Ages* (1973), 323.
141 Somerville, *History*, I, 302n.
142 G.A.J. Hodgett (ed.), *The State of Ex-Religious and Former Chantry Priests in the Diocese of Lincoln, 1547–1574* (Lincoln Rec. Soc.), 53 (Lincoln, 1959), 87.
143 *Calamy Revised*, 124.
144 ROLLR, 1D 41/34/2, p. 35.
145 ROLLR, 1D 41/18/22.
146 J. Broad (ed.), *Bishop Wake's Summary of Visitation Returns from the Diocese of Lincoln 1705–15*, II (Oxford, 2012), 735–6; Lincs. Archives, DIOC/GIBSON/4, p. 18; DIOC/GIBSON/12, p. 30.
147 Deeds of 27 Borough Street, in private hands.

arrangement broke down following the arrival of a new Wesleyan minister in c.1805, and it split into two separate schools.[148] On the initiative of the countess of Loudon and Moira, the parish church opened Sunday schools in 1809, and within four months, 91 boys and 93 girls had enrolled.[149] The strength of nonconformity in the parish is shown in 1833, when the Methodist Sunday school was attended by 124 boys and 136 girls, the Baptist by 110 boys and 99 girls and the Anglican by 100 boys and 60 girls.[150] By 1851 there was also a Sunday school attached to the Independent Chapel, attended by 84 scholars.[151]

Weekday Schools 1780–1902

There was a parish school taught by the parish clerk in 1789,[152] when it was decided to sell the 'old School house' to Mr Darbyshire and a 'poor house' to John Bakewell, to raise £100 towards the cost of a new school. The balance was met by subscriptions, including 10 guineas from the earl of Moira.[153] The churchwardens advertised for a schoolmaster in 1802, and although only reading and writing had been taught in the past, 'if the Master should chuse to teach Grammar and Latin, it would be the more desirable to the Inhabitants'.[154] The need of those ambitious parents was met separately by the opening of a boarding school in 1803 (see below). By 1818, Castle Donington also had several dame schools, which together with the parish school educated 286 children.[155] By 1833, there were two infants' schools, one founded in 1831 (with 20 children) and one in 1833 (for 90 children), with the latter partially funded by a subscription. There were also five daily schools for older children: two educating a total of 48 boys and 27 girls, and three schools formed in 1828, 1831 and 1832 attended by a total of 56 boys and 21 girls.[156]

The Methodists began a day school in the chapel vestry in 1843, with pupils charged 2d. weekly.[157] The average attendance was 60 or 70.[158] William Stenson, the Superintendent of the Baptist Sunday school, began a day school in the 1840s,[159] with accommodation for 100 children, and average attendance of 60 in 1852.[160] These schools had closed by the 1860s.

The parochial school which had opened in 1802 was 'small & inconvenient', with no playground, and the average attendance in 1852 was just 12, far less than either nonconformist school, reflecting the religious balance of the parish, and that 'few could afford the weekly fee'. Curate John Bourne (soon to become vicar) began collecting subscriptions to build a new school for 'children of the labouring poor', to accommodate

---

148 C.H. Clayton, *The History of the General Baptist Sunday School at Castle Donington* (1890), 14.
149 Town bk, 1810.
150 *Education Enquiry* (Parl. Papers 1835 (62), xlii), p. 484.
151 TNA, HO 129/444/1/12–13, 15.
152 J. Byng (C.B. Andrews, ed.), *The Torrington Diaries*, II (1935), 160.
153 Town bk, 1798–9.
154 *Leic. Jnl*, 12 Nov. 1802.
155 *Report of Select Committee on Educ. of the Poor* (Parl. Papers 1819 (224), ix), p. 45.
156 *Education Enquiry* (Parl. Papers 1835 (62), xlii), p. 484.
157 W. White, *Dir. Leics. and Rutl.* (Sheffield, 1846), 339.
158 A.H.W. Harrison, *Outlines of the History of Wesleyan Methodism in Castle Donington* (Derby, c.1904), 10.
159 White, *Dir. Leics. and Rutl.* (Sheffield, 1846), 341; not shown in Pigot & Co., *Dir. Leics. and Rutl.* (1841), 7.
160 TNA, ED 103/30.

150 boys and 150 girls, with a house for the master. A site on Castle Hill owned by Shardlow Poor Law Union was conveyed to parish trustees. The school opened in 1855, with the cost of £1,607 15s. 0d. funded by a government grant of £620 and subscriptions.[161] More places were needed in 1870 to meet the requirements of the new Education Act, but those in favour of the alternative of a non-denominational board school were prevented from giving proper notice of their meeting, which was therefore deemed 'informal'.[162] At an 'official' meeting two months later, attended by over 300 ratepayers and other property owners, the vicar produced statistics suggesting that a board school would prove more expensive than a subscription to enlarge the parochial school. On putting it to the vote, only 38 people chose the board with seven times that number against.[163] The possibility of opening a school affiliated to the British Society was separately rejected.[164] Donations totalling £325 3s. 0d. to enlarge the parochial school were collected from 50 residents of Castle Donington and local villages, headed by £50 from the countess of Loudon. With the assistance of another government grant for £158 5s. 0d., the school was extended to provide an additional 190 places.[165] The Wesleyans responded by purchasing an old hosiery factory near the junction of Delven Lane and Dovecote for £350, which was converted into a Methodist day school and opened in January 1874.[166] Although the layout was far from ideal, it was accepted by the Board of Education as a school for 276 pupils, creating a large surplus of places for a stagnant population.[167]

There was also a small school at Cavendish Bridge, built in 1859 by George Eaton, the owner of Cavendish Bridge Brewery, for the children of his workforce.[168] It had closed by 1908.[169] Another at King's Mills in the 1860s, run by the wife of the mills' manager, appears to have been short-lived.[170]

Day Schools from 1902

The Board of Education threatened to withdraw the grants to both the parochial and Wesleyan schools from 1907 unless the buildings were updated.[171] A public meeting voted in favour of trying to raise the money for both schools in preference to the imposition of a single council school largely chargeable to the rates.[172] A voluntary committee was formed to raise cash, but both boards of managers refused to make the improvements,[173] and a statutory notice was issued to build a council school with

161 TNA, ED 103/30.
162 TNA, ED 2/272, letters from Attwood, Pickering and Chapman.
163 *Derby Merc.*, 18 Jan. 1871; *School Boards* (Parl. Papers (332), 1873), p. 5.
164 ROLLR, DE 5569/2, p. 206.
165 TNA, ED 103/30.
166 TNA, ED 2/272, letter from Dunnicliffe; Harrison, *Outlines*, 14–15; CADMT, 2012.13.1.
167 TNA, ED 21/10223; *VCH Leics.*, III, 187.
168 *Derb. Chron.*, 15 Oct. 1859; *Derby Merc.*, 24 Oct. 1860.
169 *Kelly's Dir. Leics. and Rutl.* (1908), 55.
170 J.M. Lee, 'The rise and fall of a market town: Castle Donington in the nineteenth century', *Trans LAHS*, 32 (1956), 56.
171 *Derby Daily Telegraph*, 12 Oct. 1906.
172 Ibid., 18 Oct. 1906; 1 Nov. 1906.
173 *Derby Daily Telegraph*, 9 Feb. 1907; *Loughborough Monitor*, 21 Mar. 1907.

Figure 11 *The County Council Schools, built in 1910.*

450 places.[174] The managers came under pressure to change their minds when enough money was raised or guaranteed to save the existing schools, but while the Wesleyan managers held firm, the managers of the parochial schools, after lengthy prevarication, agreed on the casting vote of their acting chairman to proceed with the building work.[175] The Board of Education gave their approval, but also insisted that a council school was erected for 320 children,[176] even though only 190 children attended the Wesleyan school which would close.[177] The refurbished parochial school reopened in August 1908.[178] A fresh poll of subscribers resulted in the election of two women as foundation managers, Miss Eaton and Miss Place, alongside Gillies Shields.[179] The council school (Fig. 11) opened on Dovecote in January 1911,[180] at a cost in excess of £5,300,[181] partly met by a government grant of £1,400;[182] the architect was W.H. Hampton of Loughborough.[183] It was agreed that the board of the new county school would comprise six Anglicans and six nonconformists, with the chair taken by turn,[184] but the strength of the nonconformist

174 *Loughborough Monitor*, 7 Nov. 1907.
175 30 Jan. 1908.
176 Ibid., 13 Feb. 1908; 20 Feb. 1908.
177 TNA, ED 21/10221.
178 *Loughborough Monitor*, 4 Jun. 1908; 13 Aug. 1908.
179 Ibid., 25 Jun. 1908.
180 CADMT, 2012.13.1.
181 *Nottingham Evening Post*, 17 Oct. 1910.
182 TNA, ED 21/10221; the building is described in Ryder (2000), 7.
183 *Nottingham Evening Post*, 17 Oct. 1910.
184 Ibid., 19 Oct. 1910.

interest is demonstrated by the appointments of the headmaster and four staff from the Wesleyan school as head and as teachers at the council school.[185]

Both schools initially catered for all ages. They were reorganised by the county Education Committee in 1923, so that all children aged nine or under were taught in the school on Castle Hill, with those over nine years attending the school on Dovecote.[186] The age of transfer was increased to 11 in 1934.[187] Following the 1944 Education Act, the Dovecote building became a secondary modern school, educating children aged 11 to 15. Children who passed the 11-plus examination transferred to a grammar school in Loughborough. The secondary modern school moved to a new site for 380 pupils on Mount Pleasant in 1958, following the relaxation of post-war spending restrictions.[188] Under the 'Leicestershire Plan', which introduced comprehensive secondary education across the county, it became a high school for children aged 11–14 in 1967, with older children attending a school in Loughborough.[189] Three years later, Castle Donington became one of three trial areas in Leicestershire that moved to a four-year high school plan, with children changing schools at age 10 rather than 11.[190] The High School became a Community College in the 1970s, and when catchment areas changed in 1976, children transferred to Hind Leys College in Shepshed at the age of 14. It became an academy in 2012, withdrawn from local authority control, and in 2014 began to consult with parents with the intention of serving children aged 11 to 16.[191] In 2015 there were 422 children on the roll.[192]

The Castle Hill school became a 'Church of England controlled' primary school in 1944. When the secondary school moved in 1958, the children at Castle Hill moved into the building on Dovecote and the Castle Hill building closed.[193] St Edward's Church of England controlled primary school, which had 178 children on the roll in 2012,[194] still occupied the Dovecote building in 2015. Orchard Primary School on Grange Drive, to the north of Park Lane, was built in 1970 to provide additional primary places for the growing population,[195] and had 198 children on the roll in 2013.[196]

Boarding Schools

Miss Brellisford and Miss Wilson ran boarding schools for girls in 1811,[197] as did Miss Carr in 1814.[198] Three boarding schools for young ladies in 1828 all continued until at

185 Ibid., 13 Dec. 1910; TNA ED 21/33418 Inspection report 28 May 1925.
186 TNA, ED 21/33418, letter 10 Feb. 1923.
187 Ibid., Inspection 29 Jun. 1933.
188 Leics Educ. Committee, *The Opening of Castle Donington Secondary School* (1958).
189 http://www.castledonington.leics.sch.uk (accessed 1 Jul. 2014).
190 R.A. Illsley, 'Four years or three?' in A.N. Fairbairn (ed.), *The Leicestershire Plan* (1980), 30–43.
191 http://www.castledonington.leics.sch.uk (accessed 1 Jul. 2014).
192 http://reports.ofsted.gov.uk/report, 2015 (accessed 22 Mar. 2016).
193 ROLLR, DE 4365/295, pp. 2–3.
194 http://reports.ofsted.gov.uk/report, 2012 (accessed 22 Mar. 2016).
195 http://www.orchardprimary.org/prospectus.php (accessed 1 Jul. 2014).
196 http://reports.ofsted.gov.uk/report, 2013 (accessed 22 Mar. 2016).
197 *Derby Merc.,* 10 Jan. 1811; *Leic. Jnl,* 4 Jan. 1811.
198 *Leic. Jnl,* 7 Jan. 1814.

least 1835, run by Mrs Brown, Mrs Henshaw and the Misses Robey.[199] From 1835 the Robeys' school continued in Borough Street under the Misses Adams, and had ten female boarders aged between seven and 17 in 1841.[200] Mrs Brown's school was replaced by another boarding school in Bondgate, run by the Misses Smith.[201] In 1861, Miss Knight's seminary on Borough Street had five female boarders, aged between 11 and 14.[202] There appears to have been only one boarding school for boys. The 'Classical and Commercial' day and boarding school was opened in 1803 in a house in Borough Street by William Leeson, who had moved from Findern (Derb.),[203] and had 42 pupils in 1833.[204] By 1836 the school was run by his son, W.H. Leeson. The curriculum included English grammar, writing, arithmetic, geography, history, chronology, mensuration and mathematics; lessons in Latin, Greek, French, drawing, music and dancing were also available for an additional fee, and there was an 800-volume library.[205] The school had 24 boarders in 1841, aged between 8 and 14.[206] After Leeson's death in 1856, the school reopened under the leadership of Richard Willson, and by 1865 it had become known as the grammar school.[207] It had 11 boarders aged between 9 and 15 in 1861.[208] In 1872 it moved from Borough Street to a larger house in High Street.[209] The school closed in 1890, following the bankruptcy of proprietor Richard Willson.[210]

Major Shields offered Donington Hall to the Ockenden Venture in 1957 for children from 'Displaced Persons' Camps' in Europe. Accommodation, education and training were provided to 17 children initially, mostly boys aged 9 to 17, with numbers gradually increasing to 40. The last of the children and the staff left in 1966.[211]

Evening Schools

The Baptist church opened a writing school on Wednesday evenings in 1826,[212] and by 1833 the Anglican and Methodist Churches also provided evening writing schools.[213] These schools had closed by the 1860s. A non-denominational evening continuation school met each winter from 1893 to 1918.[214]

199 Pigot & Co., *Dir. Leics. and Rutl.* (1828), 476; (1835), 115.
200 *Derby Merc.*, 1 Jul. 1835, p. 3; TNA, HO 107/594/24.
201 Pigot & Co., *Dir. Leics. and Rutl.* (1841), 7; White, *Dir. Leics. and Rutl.* (Sheffield, 1846), 340–1.
202 TNA, RG 9/2487.
203 *Derby Merc.*, 13 Jan. 1803.
204 *Education Enquiry* (Parl. Papers 1835 (62), xlii), p. 484.
205 *Derby Merc.*, 6 Jan. 1836.
206 TNA, HO 107/594/24.
207 *Derby Merc*, 3 Sept. 1856, 14 Jan. 1857, 11 Jan. 1865.
208 TNA, RG 9/2487.
209 *Derby Merc.*, 24 Jan. 1872.
210 *London Gaz.*, 21 Feb. 1890, 997; *Derby Daily Telegraph*, 10 Dec. 1890.
211 TNA, BN 62/3145.
212 Clayton, *The History*, 22.
213 *Education Enquiry* (Parl. Papers 1835 (62), xlii), p. 484.
214 ROLLR, DE 5569/6.

RELIGIOUS HISTORY

A PRIEST IS MENTIONED IN Domesday Book,[1] although the first firm evidence for a church is from *c.*1134, when it was given by William FitzNigel to his foundation of Runcorn (later Norton) priory.[2] The dedication to the Anglo-Saxon 'St Edward' is documented in 1301, and may suggest an early foundation.[3] The earliest evidence of the full dedication is from 1490, when St Edward, king and martyr, was recorded.[4] The building largely dates from the 13th and early 14th centuries.

Donington's location near the borders of three counties and three dioceses, combined with its distant lords and a market, allowed religious pluralism to develop early. Lollard views were expressed in the early 15th century, and by the late 17th century there were several dissenting meetings. Ejected ministers in the locality helped these congregations to flourish. Although they faded in the 18th century, they were replaced by New Connexion General Baptists and Wesleyan Methodists who both outnumbered Anglicans in their church attendance in 1851. In 2015, regular services were held in the village by the Anglican, Methodist, Baptist and Roman Catholic churches.

Parochial Organization

The seat of the Mercian diocese of Leicester was moved to Dorchester-on-Thames (Oxon.) in the 870s and to Lincoln in *c.*1072,[5] and any Anglo-Saxon church in Castle Donington would have looked to the bishops of that diocese. The parish remained in Lincoln diocese until transferred to Peterborough diocese in 1837,[6] and then to the newly formed Leicester diocese in 1926.[7] The ecclesiastical parish was extended in 1987 to include Lockington cum Hemington.[8]

---

1   *Domesday*, 632.
2   J. Tait (ed.), 'The foundation charter of Runcorn (later Norton) priory' (Chetham Society, n.s. 100, Manchester, 1939), 19; *VCH Ches.* III, 165.
3   TNA, DL 25/1771.
4   TNA, DL 30/80/1091, m. 2.
5   A.W. Haddan and W. Stubbs (eds.), *Councils and Ecclesiastical Documents relating to Great Britain and Ireland*, III (Oxford, 1871), 129; D.M. Owen, 'Introduction: the English church in eastern England, 1066–1100', in D.M. Owen (ed.), *The History of Lincoln Minster* (Cambridge, 1994), 10.
6   *London Gaz.* 12 Sept. 1837, 2397–8.
7   *London Gaz.* 12 Nov. 1926, 7321–2.
8   *Leic. Dioc. Dir.*, 1987–8, 67.

Advowson

The advowson formed part of the endowment of William, baron of Halton, to his foundation of Runcorn (later Norton) Priory before 1134, and the living was formally appropriated by the priory in 1331.[9] After the dissolution in 1536,[10] the advowson was sold in 1545 to Robert Lawrence and William Symson, together with the rectory and Wavertoft land.[11] They passed together through several hands,[12] including the earls of Huntingdon between 1553 and 1588, until settled on John Manners (later 8th earl of Rutland) in 1628.[13] Manners sold the rectory and advowson to Henry Markham in 1652, and these remained in the Markham family for more than a century. Sir Richard Adams, nephew and heir of Esther Markham, sold them in 1766 to Samuel Follows, merchant of Castle Donington, for £5,000. Follows sold to Leonard Fosbrooke in 1769.[14] Fosbrooke sold the advowson to Clement Winstanley in 1786, who sold it to Charles Curtis the following year, who sold to Joseph Harding in 1790. In 1802 it returned to the Hastings family through purchase by the earl of Moira, and descended with the park estate into the 20th century.[15] Major Gretton purchased the advowson in 1903,[16] and it subsequently passed by inheritance. In 1987, when the parish was extended to include Lockington cum Hemington, John Curzon was added for the Lockington cum Hemington interest.[17] Jennifer, Lady Gretton became patron for the Donington interest in 1992,[18] and continued to hold the advowson in 2015.

Income

The tax of 10 marks paid by the church in the 1250s was the median figure for the deanery.[19] The value of the living was £17 6s. 8d. in 1291, with a pension of £2 13s. 4d. to Norton priory.[20] A portion was reserved for the vicar when the rectory was appropriated by Norton priory in 1331,[21] and licence was obtained in 1343 to reserve 60s. of income each year for the bishop of Lincoln.[22] The living was valued at £8 2s. 3½d. in 1535, one of the lowest in the deanery.[23]

---

9   *Cal. Papal Reg.* II, 379; *Cal. Pat.* 1330–4, 88–9.
10   *VCH Ches.* III, 171.
11   *L. & P. Hen. VIII*, XX (2), p. 216; *HMC Hastings I*, p. 35.
12   Above, 40.
13   ROLLR, 4D 42/34.
14   Derb. RO, D1336/1/18/2–5.
15   *Derby Merc.*, 23 Feb. 1786; Derb. RO, D1336/1/18/6–13.
16   *Benefices Act 1898* (Parl. Papers, 1904 (366), LXXIV), p. 50.
17   *Leic. Dioc. Dir.*, 1987–8, 67.
18   *Leic. Dioc. Dir.*, 1992, 64.
19   W.P.W. Phillimore (ed.), *Rotuli Hugonis de Welles, Episcopi Lincolniensis* (1909), I, 278.
20   *Tax. Eccl.*, 64.
21   *Cal. Papal Reg.* II, 379; *Cal. Pat.* 1330–4, 88–9.
22   *Cal. Pat.* 1343–5, 130.
23   *Valor Eccl.*, IV, 177–9.

The vicarage estate in 1601 comprised 2 a. of land at the parsonage, 12 a. in the open fields, meadow yielding six loads of hay, five beast pastures, two groat pastures (costing 4d. annually) and 25 sheep commons.[24] The vicar's tithes recorded in 1707 included moduses for the ferry and fishing, horses and cattle, with pigs and lambs paid in kind.[25] The parishioners obtained written acknowledgement from the vicar in 1683 that if his tithe lambs were still suckling after May Day it was no more than 'a neybourly Courtesye'.[26] The redistribution of clerical incomes under the Interregnum resulted in an award to the vicar in 1659.[27] The yearly value of the vicarage in 1711 was certified as £33 1s., and the living was discharged from further payments of first fruits and tenths.[28] An augmentation of £200 was made from Queen Anne's Bounty in 1722, against a benefaction of like amount from John Hardinge,[29] of King's Newton (Derb.), and used to purchase land in Castle Donington.[30] At inclosure in 1779, the vicar received 52 a. for the glebe land, and income, worth £43 7s. that year, from a further 30 a. held jointly with the lay impropriator, in lieu of small tithes.[31] Moduses continued to be paid on 'ancient' inclosures and the fishery, including 10s. for Donington Park and 9s. 11¼d. for the former priory closes at Wavertoft.[32] With the exception of the fishing, these became rent charges in 1848.[33] The annual income from the living was said to be under £200 in 1789, 'but capable of improvement'.[34] In 1873, gross income of £223 was recorded, which had reduced to £165 by 1907.[35]

Parsonage

The parsonage grounds fronted the market place, and contained a substantial house of five bays in 1696, with a barn, stable and coal house.[36] In 1765 there were five lodging chambers, three garrets, two cock lofts, a barn of two bays, two stables, a cow house and a coal house.[37] The house was 'in pretty good repair' in 1775,[38] but rain was entering in 1797.[39] By 1821, vicar John Dalby had 'taken down, enlarged and rebuilt the West end of the house, partly rebuilt the East end, taken off the Roof of the remainder, raised the Walls, and covered the whole with slates and tiles, added a small hall at the back, erected two new staircases, made a cellar and put down a leaden pump', at his own expense.[40] The

24   Lincs. Archives, DIOC/TER 13/50.
25   Lincs. Archives, DIOC/TER/23, pp. 265–71.
26   Town bk, 1682.
27   Lambeth Palace Libr., COMM VIa/10, p. 23; COMM VII/2, p. 164.
28   J. Ecton, *Liber Valorum et Decimarum* (1711), 210.
29   C. Hodgson, *An Account of the Augmentation of Small Livings* (1845), cxxxvi.
30   CERC, QAB/7/5/K6066.
31   ROLLR, DE 5251/1.
32   Lincs. Archives, DIOC/TER BUNDLE/LEICS/ CASTLE DONINGTON, 1821.
33   TNA, IR 18/4412.
34   *Derby Merc.*, 18 Jun. 1789.
35   *Peterborough Dioc. Cal., Clergy List and Almanac* 1873, 37; *1907*, 144.
36   ROLLR, PR/I/101/82.
37   Lincs. Archives, DIOC/TER BUNDLE/LEICS/DONINGTON CASTLE, 176.
38   ROLLR, 1D 41/18/21, p. 15.
39   ROLLR, 1D 41/18/22, p. 15.
40   Lincs. Archives, PD 163/32; DIOC/TER BUNDLE/LEICS/DONINGTON CASTLE, 1821.

house was sold in the early 1980s, and a new house built for the vicar just to its east, with an entrance from Delven Lane.

Great Tithes

The great tithes were paid to Norton priory until the dissolution, and then to lay impropriators, descending with the advowson and the former abbey lands until 1786. They may have been let for the whole of this period, with known farmers including Robert Roby and Francis Thomasman in 1689,[41] and John Lacy in 1774.[42] When Donington was inclosed in 1779, Leonard Fosbrooke received 220 a. 3 r. 28 p. in compensation for the extinguished great tithes, excluding the 30 a. allotted jointly with the vicar, where Fosbrooke was entitled to the capital value.[43] The tithe allotment was subsequently divided into 19 closes, let to five tenants, and placed on the market in 1786.[44] By 1831, the Fosbrooke family held no land in the parish.[45]

Religious Life before the Reformation

Pastoral Care and Lollardy

There was a priest in Donington in 1086. There would have been another at the hospital from its foundation, there was a chaplain at the castle by 1220,[46] and by 1301 there was a priest serving the 'St Mary' guild.[47] Six priests paid the clerical poll taxes in 1381.[48] A papal indult of 1399 provided for future vicars to be canons from Norton,[49] and at some stage the priory's arms were added to the east window.[50] The vicars may have provided little clerical guidance to inhabitants, as Lollard opinions were expressed openly in the early 15th century. John Seynour, a presumed Lollard, was required to go to Canterbury to abjure his heresy in c.1403,[51] and shoemaker John Anneys was alleged in 1413 to have preached heresy in taverns. Anneys was said to be a follower of a Lollard named William, tentatively identified as William Ederick of Aston-on-Trent (Derb.), a prominent Lollard who was harboured by Thomas and Agnes Tickhill,[52] and was almost certainly 'William Tykelprest', who had preached at Castle Donington the previous Easter, with the consent of the parishioners.[53]

41   Town bk, 1689.
42   ROLLR, QS 62/71.
43   ROLLR, DE 5251/1.
44   *Derby Merc.*, 23 Feb. 1786.
45   ROLLR, DE 253 (a) (ii).
46   Phillimore (ed.), *Rotuli Hugonis*, I, 252.
47   TNA, DL 25/1771.
48   A.K. McHardy, *Clerical Poll-Taxes of the Diocese of Lincoln, 1377–1381* (Lincoln Rec. Soc., 81, Lincoln, 1992), 17.
49   *Cal. Papal Reg.* V, 186.
50   Burton, 84.
51   I. Forrest, *The Detection of Heresy in Late Medieval England* (Oxford, 2005), 132, 146.
52   J. Crompton, 'Leicestershire Lollards', *Trans. LAHS,* 44 (1968–9), 27–8, 40–41.
53   Forrest, *Detection of Heresy*, 216–7.

Five priests were listed in a tax assessment of 1526: Dr Cliff, the vicar, had an income of £8, chantry priest John Dagull had a stipend of £6 6s. 8d., two other priests had stipends of £4 13s. 4d. each, and one had no stipend. The vicar was almost certainly not resident, as he was also the bishop of Ely's Chancellor,[54] but no curate is named, and the other priests may have shared the duties between them. Dagull may have been the hospital chaplain, as he left 12d. in his will in 1533 'to every brother of the house'.[55] There were no residents remaining in the hospital in 1545.[56] Two Donington residents left bequests to friaries in Derby and Nottingham,[57] but there is no evidence that friars visited.

Guild and Chantries

A gift of rent in 1301 mentions a chapel within the church which was dedicated to St Mary, with its own priest, John Lakator.[58] The date corresponds to architectural evidence of substantial work at the east end of the south aisle in the late 13th or early 14th century. Four more grants over the next four years, including one in 1304 by William le Verniz 'for the service of St Mary' suggest this was a parish guild, rather than a private chantry.[59] A tomb recess was created in the chancel at about the same time as the chapel was created, which contains a slightly later priest's effigy of c.1320–30,[60] perhaps the guild's first priest. Freeholder John Lacatour held land in Donington equivalent to one-tenth of a knight's fee,[61] paid lay taxes in 1327 and 1332,[62] and possibly paid for this tomb.

A survey of 1462 lists one and a half burgages and two cottages held by 'the wardens of the church and light of St Mary' and an acre of land held by Edward Kettell known as 'Gyldelandes'.[63] A further gift of copyhold property in the long row on the green was made in 1490 to the churchwarden and warden of the light of the blessed Mary.[64] A 'St Mary priest' continued to be employed until 1540 when, perhaps driven at least in part by reformers in the parish, the income for the priest had been diverted to secular needs. William Newbury explained in 1550 that 'the inhabitants' had previously hired a priest for the benefit of the whole town, giving him one sheaf from every land, but that had proved insufficient, so 'the town' agreed that five tenements should be held by the vicar and churchwardens (possibly the gift in 1490), with the rental income used to pay for a priest, unless there were more pressing church repairs or legal suits for the liberties of the inhabitants. It may be no coincidence that a number of law suits were taken to the Duchy

---

54   H. Salter (ed.), *A Subsidy Collected in the Diocese of Lincoln in 1526* (Oxford, 1909), 111; A.P. Moore, 'Proceedings of the ecclesiastical courts in the Archdeaconry of Leicester, 1516–35', *Assoc. Archit. Soc. Rep. & Papers*, 28 (1905–6), 192.

55   ROLLR, Will reg. 1526-33/75.

56   M.E.C. Walcott, 'Chantries of Leicestershire and the inventory of Olneston', *Assoc. Archit. Soc. Rep. & Papers*, 10 (1870–1), 332.

57   ROLLR, Will reg. 1515-26/58; 1515-26/468.

58   TNA, DL 25/1771.

59   TNA, DL 25/1773.

60   A. Hamilton Thompson, 'An account of the church', *Trans. LAHS*, 14 (1925–6), 79.

61   TNA, C 135/24/40; C 135/119/61.

62   TNA, E 179/133/1, rot. 12; E179/133/2 rot. 1d.

63   TNA, DL 43/6/3; Farnham 56–63.

64   TNA, DL 30/80/1091, m. 2.

conciliar court in this period, involving steward Thomas Grey. Newbury's claim that in 1550 there had been no 'St Mary priest' for a decade was disputed by John Gatley.[65]

A licence to endow a chantry to the annual value of 10 marks was granted to Harold Staunton and Thomas Hesilrige in 1511.[66] In his will of 1513, Staunton directed that lands to this value were to be purchased for this purpose in Billesdon,[67] two chalices were to be purchased and a bell was to be rung before the celebration, 'that labourers and wayfaring menne may cum to his masse'. The chantry priest was also to teach grammar, and Staunton left a further £10 for books and for the ornamentation of the high altar.[68] No will has been found for Thomas Hesilrige. He may have left money for the altar to St Thomas within the church, recorded in 1537.[69]

Religious Life after the Reformation

Dissolution of the Guild and Chantry

Robert Thomas and Andrew Salter, merchant tailors of London, bought 4 a. of land, 1 a. of meadow and five cottages in Castle Donington from the crown in 1550, which had been given to support a priest in the parish church, including a property abutting the church porch. A property known as the 'Saint Marye house', which may have been the one abutting the church porch, was occupied by Thomas Grey (II) from 1578 until at least 1584, together with another house and 5 a. land that had originally been given to support the 'St Marye priest'.[70] When the Staunton chantry was dissolved in 1547 it held four messuages with their lands in Billesdon, let for £7 18s., and a chantry house and buildings in Donington, worth £8 4s. 8d. annually.[71] Lands in Billesdon and rents of £1 4s. 2d. in Billesdon and Castle Donington, possessions of 'the late chantry', were purchased from the crown by Robert Catlyn in 1550.[72]

Under the heading 'Chantry House', Nichols describes two houses: one on the south side of the churchyard whose gable was decorated with a plaster bust and two shields displaying the arms of the Company of Plaisterers, and one 'called the Chantry-house … adjoining to Atkins' entry', but gives no other indication where this was.[73] The former appears to be the house with a 'quaint old gable' projecting into the churchyard, described by trade directories as a 'chantry house',[74] and was probably the 'St Mary House'. It was dismissed by architect W. Pearson as 'nothing more than the "frame and

65   TNA, DL 3/56/G5f.
66   *L & P Henry VIII*, I (1), p. 420.
67   TNA, PROB 11/17/257.
68   TNA, PROB 11/17/257.
69   ROLLR, W&I file 1537/37.
70   TNA, DL 44/349.
71   A. Hamilton Thompson, 'The Chantry Certificates for Leicestershire', *Assoc. Archit. Soc. Rep. & Papers*, 30 (1909–10), 504–5.
72   *Cal. Pat.* Edw. VI, III, 124.
73   Nichols, III, 780.
74   W. White, *Dir. Leics. and Rutl.* (Sheffield, 1877), 183.

pane" domestic architecture common in the middle-class houses of that period',[75] and was demolished in 1872.[76]

Pastoral Care and Religious Life

The churchwardens' accounts show the removal of the medieval stone altars in 1550 and the sale of the holy water stoup in 1551. Painted glass might also have been destroyed, as a glazier from Burton-upon-Trent was paid 8s. 8d. in 1550 to re-glaze the widows. After the restoration of Catholicism by Queen Mary, the parish paid John Parker 20d. in 1555 for making a cross for the rood, and paid a plumber for a replacement lead, or lead-lined, stoup. The following year John Parker made two candlesticks for the rood loft, and various items including a cross, vestments and candlesticks were purchased from Robert Osborn, who had bought them from Simon Fox, a former churchwarden. The custom of keeping watch over a sepulchre for the two nights before Easter was introduced or, more likely, reinstated.[77]

Cardinal Pole was the uncle of the 2nd earl of Huntingdon's wife and, during Mary's reign, the earl's household outwardly professed Catholicism,[78] but the future 3rd earl was brought up as a Protestant. He became a devout Calvinist,[79] and as patron of the living presented Peter Wood as vicar in 1571, a man 'understanding the latine tong and competentlie learned in the scriptures'.[80] Wood was presented for not wearing the surplice in 1604, although the case was dismissed when he conformed.[81] Puritan nominations continued after the earl sold the advowson in 1588. In 1633, the church font was found to have no cover, the minister's seat for reading the service was in 'the middle space of the Church', and the communion table was in the nave rather than the chancel.[82] The Easter communion service in 1644 was held in the afternoon, with ale substituted for wine.[83]

Vicar Thomas Smith had been ordained by the Wirksworth (Derb.) classis in 1656. He appears to have encouraged Christian charity, and the parish collection of £12 15s. 3d. for Protestants driven out of Piedmont was the largest from any Leicestershire parish.[84] Smith refused to accept the 1662 Act of Uniformity, and became a nonconformist minister upon ejection.[85] When he left, the church had neither a Book of Common Prayer nor a surplice.[86] Smith was licensed to hold dissenting worship in the parish

75   W. Pearson, *Medieval History and Antiquities of Castle Donington* (Leicester, 1862), 8.

76   *Leic. Jnl*, 12 Jul. 1872.

77   Huntington Libr., Misc. 8/2 (microfilm copy at ROLLR).

78   C. Cross, *The Puritan Earl: The Life of Henry Hastings, Third Earl of Huntingdon, 1536–1595* (1966), 7–8, 22.

79   Ibid., 12–15, 24.

80   Ibid., 136; C.W. Foster (ed.), *The state of the church in the reigns of Elizabeth and James I, as illustrated by documents relating to the Diocese of Lincoln*, I (Lincoln Rec. Soc. 23, Lincoln, 1926), 33, 108.

81   Foster (ed.), *State of the Church*, cxxxii.

82   ROLLR, 1D 41/18/7, f. 1v.

83   W. Dugdale, *A Short View of the Late Troubles in England* (1681), 569–70.

84   O. Cromwell, *A Distinct and Faithful Accompt of all the Receipts for the relief of the Protestants in Piedmont* (1658), 41–3; Town bk, 1658, quotes £13 8s. 10d.

85   *Calamy Revised*, 449.

86   A.P. Moore, 'The primary visitation of Robert Sanderson, bishop of Lincoln, in 1662, for the Archdeaconry of Leicester', *The Antiquary* (1909), 224.

in 1672,[87] and it is likely that several parishioners followed him. Vicar George Gell, instituted in 1704,[88] had some success at rebuilding a congregation. Forty families did not attend church in 1709,[89] but by 1721 there were only 20 families of dissenters, most of whom occasionally conformed.[90]

Nonconformity grew rapidly from the 1750s, when the vicarage was largely held by two John Dalbys, uncle from 1758–80 and nephew from 1807–52. Attendances of 173 people in the morning and 202 in the afternoon on census Sunday in 1851 are unimpressive in a settlement of 3,028 people,[91] and dwarfed by the 402 people attending the evening service that day at the Wesleyan church,[92] and the congregation of 302 people at the evening service in the Baptist church, both following earlier services that day.[93] Vicar John Bourne estimated in 1872 that about 40 per cent of his parishioners were dissenters.[94] Although he adopted an ecumenical outlook, patronised united services,[95] and regularly attracted congregations of 300–350 in the morning and 450–500 in the evening, he admitted the church had no more than 35 communicants, even at festivals.[96]

The church dedication was changed during the incumbency of the second John Dalby, perhaps in an attempt to reach out to those who considered a non-Biblical saint to be akin to 'Popery'. The dedication to St Edward held until the early 1840s,[97] but Reverend Dalby claimed on the 1851 religious census that the church was 'not called by any particular name'.[98] Almost all trade directories from 1846 until the 1920s give the dedication as St Luke,[99] as does the Ordnance Survey. By the 1870s, the date of the October hiring fair was said to have been determined by 'Old St Luke's Day' (29 October),[100] creating the erroneous impression that the dedication to St Luke was longstanding. High church views gained ground in the early 20th century, and the church became St Edward, King and Martyr again from the late 1920s.[101]

Fixtures, Fittings and Restoration

A raised tomb of grey marble near the south door is topped by brasses of Robert Staunton (steward 1485–93) and his wife Agnes, lying under crocketed canopies. It appears to have been created in Robert Staunton's lifetime, as it leaves a blank space

87   *Cal. SP Dom.* May–Sept. 1672, 62; 1672–3, 93.
88   Lincs. Archives, Subscription bk VI.
89   J. Broad (ed.), *Bishop Wake's Summary of Visitation Returns from the Diocese of Lincoln 1705–15*, II (Oxford, 2012), 736.
90   Lincs. Archives, DIOC/GIBSON/12, p. 30.
91   TNA, HO 129/444/11.
92   TNA, HO 129/444/13.
93   TNA, HO 129/444/1/15.
94   Northants RO, ML 594.
95   *Derby Telegraph*, 5 Feb. 1859; 26 Jan.1861; 7 Jan. 1863.
96   Northants RO, ML 594.
97   Nichols, III, 781; Pigot, *Dir. Leics. and Rutl.* (1835), 115; Pigot, *Dir. Leics. and Rutl.* (1841), 7.
98   TNA, HO 129/444/11.
99   White adhered to St Edward in 1863 and gives both in 1877: White *Dir. Leics. and Rutl.* (Sheffield, 1863), 485, (Sheffield, 1877), 182 .
100   W. White, *Dir. Leics. and Rutl.* (Sheffield, 1877), 182.
101   Trade directories.

for the date he died.[102] The monument stood in the middle of the south chapel in 1675, by a step to the altar,[103] but was moved near the south door in the 20th century. At the east end of the north aisle a chest tomb bears the alabaster effigies of Robert Haselrigge (steward 1517–c.1535) and his wife Eleanor. These were said to have been richly gilded, but the gilt was wearing off in 1675,[104] and none remains. Around the sides are figures of bedesmen and angels bearing shields carrying the arms of Haselrigge, Staunton and Shirley.[105] Carvings on the west and east ends are badly defaced, and may have been the Virgin and the Trinity.[106]

Frequent post-Reformation changes in lay rector may have contributed to neglect of the chancel, which was in poor condition in 1633. The battlements over the east end were loose and those on the north had fallen down. Windows elsewhere, and the clock, were broken.[107] The work appears to have been put in hand soon after, and in 1663 the spire of 180 feet was also partly rebuilt. A brave manorial jury of 13 people 'Clymed upp by lathers from the Bartlements' to inspect the work.[108] In 1702, the Markham family, lay rectors, agreed to give the earl of Huntingdon a seat in the chancel in exchange for the third seat behind the central pulpit.[109] Mrs Markham asked the earl to remove his two pews from the chancel in 1738,[110] possibly as part of a restoration. Expenditure between 1769 and 1771 aimed at repairing, 'beautifying' and 'ornamenting' the church,[111] and the fabric was judged sound in 1775 and 1797.[112] A 'few select Passages of Scripture' were painted on the walls.[113] North and west galleries and a central pulpit and reading desk, were recorded in 1833 and survived until the restoration of 1875 (Fig. 12).[114]

By 1832, the chancel was 'in a most dangerous state', with a large crack running down the east wall, and the window 'ready to fall in'.[115] Repairs were completed by 1835,[116] but the remainder of the church was 'a disgusting spectacle', with the paved floor collapsing 'down to the skeletons of the bodies underneath'. With a population in excess of 3,000, 'two-thirds of which are comprised in a class too indigent to contribute a shilling', the vicar sought a grant from the Incorporated Church Building Society to add more free seats, by filling all the aisles with benches. A grant of £100 was agreed and paid, despite only 180 new sittings being created rather than the 300 proposed.[117] Little more was done, and in 1862 an ecclesiologist criticised the church's 'high-backed pews, unsightly galleries, mutilated columns, whitewashed walls, blocked-up arches, and debased

102 Nichols, III, opp. 782.
103 Huntington Libr., HAM 8/19.
104 Huntington Libr., HAM 8/19.
105 Ibid.; Burton, 84.
106 Huntington Libr., HAM 8/19.
107 ROLLR, 1D 41/18/7, ff. 1v, 2.
108 Town bk, 1663.
109 Town bk.
110 ROLLR, 14D 32/394.
111 Town bk, 1769, 1770, 1771.
112 ROLLR, 1D 41/18/16–17.
113 ROLLR, 1850'245/1, pp. 81–8.
114 CADMT; Lambeth Palace Libr., ICBS 1597, f. 10.
115 ROLLR, 1850'245/1, pp. 81–8.
116 ROLLR, 1850'245/50/6, p. 31.
117 Lambeth Palace Libr., ICBS 1597; MB 7, pp. 73–4.

Figure 12 *Interior of St Edward's church before restoration in 1875.*

windows'.[118] Restoration of the church, with the exception of the chancel, began in 1875 under architect William Smith, and was completed in 1877 at a total cost of £3,847.[119] The galleries were taken down, the organ moved from the tower arch to the west end of the north aisle, and the box pews, reading desk and central pulpit removed, the latter replaced by a new pulpit to the south-east of the nave given in memory of former vicar John Dalby (II), made from bath stone, red marble and six panels cut from two or three late 15th- or early 16th-century incised alabaster monumental slabs taken from within the building.[120] The chancel was restored in 1902.[121]

There were three bells in 1552, and five by 1875,[122] including one cast in 1412. They were recast and augmented to six in 1880,[123] and a new clock and chimes added. The

118 W. Pearson, 'Paper on the mediaeval history and antiquities of Castle Donington', read to the British Arch. Assoc. (1862), 9 (copy at ROLLR).
119 Lambeth Palace Libr., ICBS 7925; MB 21, pp. 135, 325; documents in the Church records cabinet, Castle Donington.
120 *Derby Merc.*, 21 Feb. 1877.; F.A. Greenhill, *The Incised Slabs of Leics. and Rutl.* (Leicester, 1958), 64–5.
121 *Kelly's Dir. Leics. and Rutl.* (1908), 55.
122 T. North, *The Church Bells of Leicestershire* (1876), 159–60.
123 E. Morris, 'Church Bells of Leicester' (unpub. n.d.), online at https://www.le.ac.uk/lahs/Bells.html (accessed 15 Jan. 2015).

bells were rehung in 1923,[124] and 1977.[125] A few fragments of medieval glass remain, but not the armorial windows to Staunton, Haselrigge and Shirley, which survived until at least the early 19th century.[126] Two modern stained glass windows by renowned artists are worthy of note, the east window of 1902 by Charles Kempe in memory of Thomas Clark and Mary Ann Souter, and the window nearest the door in the south aisle by Patrick Pollen, in memory of John Dalby, who died in 1957.

Protestant Nonconformity

No return was made to the religious census of 1676,[127] but there was probably more than one group meeting in Donington at that date. These early congregations appear to have faded away in the early 18th century. Selina, countess of Huntingdon was very influential in the formation of nonconformist churches in the locality, but appears to have had little direct impact within the parish, although New Connexion General Baptists and Wesleyans appear from the 1750s. Their congregations had become the largest in the village by 1851, and still met in 2015.

Society of Friends (Quakers)

John Evatt of Castle Donington was one of 25 Quakers imprisoned in Leicester gaol in 1660 for refusing to swear oaths.[128] Evatt, John Hood, Richard Newcomb and Thomas Glover all had crops seized for refusing to pay tithes in 1678 and 1679,[129] as did others in the later 17th and 18th centuries.[130] Evatt was fined £10 for holding a meeting in 1679, Thomas Glover and William Howett were each fined 5s. for being present and Howett was fined an additional £10 for 'the pretended property' of Evatt. An inventory was taken of Evatt's possessions, and they were all sold for 7s., although said to be worth 30 times that sum.[131] After paying the money, the sympathetic purchasers left the goods with him.[132] Another meeting in 1684 in the house of Dorothy Evatt resulted in the seizure of goods worth 18s. from her, £5 from Thomas Glover, £30 from Richard Newcomb and £6 from Isaac Gisburne of Kegworth. Newcomb was left without even a bed, dish or spoon, and he, his wife and children were obliged to lodge with a neighbour. Gisburne was fined a further £15 for preaching, but with insufficient goods, sympathetic parish officers paid the informers from their own pockets.[133]

Collections were taken at Quaker meetings across the county in 1697 and 1698 to cover the costs of raising the walls of Richard Newcomb's barn in Castle Donington and

---

124 *Kelly's Dir. Leics. and Rutl.* (1941), 54.
125 *Ringing World*, 14 Apr. 1978.
126 Burton, 84; Nichols, III, 781.
127 A. Whiteman, *The Compton Census of 1676: A Critical Edition* (1986), 306.
128 J. Besse, *A collection of the sufferings of the people called Quakers* (1753), 331–2.
129 ROLLR, 12D 39/34, f. 1.
130 Ibid., ff. 1, 54v and 103.
131 Ibid., ff.. 2–3.
132 Town bk, 1679.
133 Besse, *A collection*, 345.

fitting it out as a meeting house.[134] This is probably the house sold by Thomas Coke and John Hardinge to John Evatt and Edward Mugleston (as trustees) in 1718, together with a 'parcel of pasture called the graveyard' in Barroon.[135] Between 1706 and 1721 (and probably far longer) meetings were held every Sunday and Thursday.[136] There were ten Quaker families in Donington in 1709,[137] although this number had reduced to five by 1721, some of whom reputedly 'always' went to church.[138] Donington's Quakers included Ruth Follows, who later travelled extensively through Britain as a minister for her faith. She died at home in Castle Donington in 1808.[139]

A new meeting house with a burial ground in Barholme Street (renamed Barroon) was registered in 1829 (Fig. 13),[140] on land given by basket-maker Joseph Evatt.[141] It cost £450,[142] and could accommodate 200 people. Attendance on 30 March 1851 was just 19 in the morning and 12 in the afternoon, although 10 people were said to have been indisposed.[143] The meeting was discontinued in 1915.[144] The meeting house was let to the War Office during the Second World War,[145] and to the Church of England for five years from 1952 for use as a church hall.[146] The 'derelict' building was sold in 1959,[147] and converted to a two-storey private house.[148]

Presbyterians and Congregationalists

Donington's former vicar Thomas Smith was licensed in 1672 to preach at Presbyterian meetings in the house of Frank Thomasman in Castle Donington and Congregational meetings in Thomasman's house at Wanliff Grange (probably Wartoft Grange).[149] Samuel Wright was also licensed to preach at both Presbyterian and Congregational meetings at his house in Castle Donington.[150] William Smith, the former vicar of Packington, was licensed in 1672 to preach at both Presbyterian and Congregational meetings at his house, Diseworth Grange,[151] an unknown property and perhaps a deliberately confusing alternative name for Wartoft Grange. Smith's property was within the parish of Castle Donington, as manorial and parish officers were fined in 1681 for failing to act when an

134 ROLLR, 12D 39/1, ff. 60–66.
135 Melb. Hall Est. Office, X94/39/1/2.
136 Broad (ed.), *Bishop Wake's Summary*, 735–6; Lincs. Archives, DIOC/GIBSON/4, p. 18; DIOC/GIBSON/12, p. 30.
137 Broad (ed.), *Bishop Wake's summary*, 735–6.
138 Lincs. Archives, DIOC/GIBSON/12, p. 30.
139 *ODNB*, s.v. 'Follows, Ruth (1718–1808)', accessed 15 Jul. 2013.
140 ROLLR, QS 44/1/2.
141 Notts. Archives, NC/Q 208/2.
142 W. White, *Dir. Leics. and Rutl.* (Sheffield, 1846), 339.
143 TNA, HO 129/444/1/14.
144 D.M. Butler, *The Quaker Meeting-Houses of Britain* (1999), 354.
145 https://www.flickr.com/photos/qmh/2052436288 (accessed 11 May 2014).
146 Notts. Archives, NC/Q 208/5.
147 ROLLR, DE 3115/74.
148 RCHME, *Nonconformist Chapels and Meeting Houses in Central England* (1986), 120.
149 *Cal. SP Dom.*, May–Sept. 1672, 62; 1672–3, 93.
150 Ibid., 62, 574.
151 *Cal. SP Dom.*, 1671–2, 551; May–Sept. 1672, 62.

Figure 13 *Clockwise from top left: Wesleyan Methodist (1905), General Baptist (1774), Quaker (1829) and Independent (1840). See Map 5 for locations.*

unlawful conventicle was held there,[152] and his burial at Diseworth in 1686 records that he was 'of the parish of Castle-Donington'.[153]

Presbyterian meetings in Donington were attracting 120 hearers in 1705, including 16 men who qualified for the vote, and preacher William Walton was receiving £5 from the Common Fund for his work.[154] They had a meeting house where they assembled on Sunday afternoons, generally after attending the parish church in the morning. It was probably owned by Walton, who left a building 'called a meeting house' to his sons in his will of 1749, for use by Presbyterians.[155] Regular preachers included Walton and Mr

152 Town bk, 1680.
153 *Calamy Revised*, 450; ROLLR, DE 726/2.
154 Dr Williams's Libr., MS 34.4, f. 64.
155 ROLLR, DG8/30.

Crompton and Edmund Coalton, both of Derby.[156] In 1718 vicar George Gell recorded 30 families of dissenters 'of Presbyterian and Independent persuasion',[157] but their meetings seem to have attracted hearers with a range of religious views. Two of the three meetings held in Castle Donington in 1718 were described as 'Presbyterian-Independent-Baptist' and 'Presbyterian-Independent-Quaker'.[158]

Baptists

A conventicle of about 80 Baptists, 'most of them women and children', met at the house and barn of husbandman John Pim in 1669, during divine service or 'in the night', guided by King of Coventry and yeoman Elias Boyar of Rempstone (Notts).[159] James Harris's house had been licensed for Baptist services by 1706,[160] but meetings ceased to be held by 1715 and the family attended the parish church.[161] A 'Presbyterian-Independent-Baptist' congregation is mentioned in 1718,[162] but appears to have faded away.

New Connexion General Baptists

The New Connexion General Baptists in north-west Leicestershire owe their origins to David Taylor, servant to the countess of Huntingdon.[163] A congregation met in Castle Donington at the home of shopkeeper Samuel Follows from 1752,[164] and was a daughter congregation to the meeting encouraged by Taylor at Barton-in-the-Beans.[165] A chapel was built in 1774 on the west side of Bondgate (Fig. 13) on land given by John Bakewell senior of Church Farm.[166] It was enlarged in 1827,[167] and had 175 members in 1829.[168] The interior had galleries on three sides supported on iron columns, with a pulpit and organ on the fourth side.[169] There was a minister's house and Sunday school to the north, with a small burial ground at the front, and another to the rear. Baptisms took place in the river Trent until 1839, when a baptistery was created in the church.[170] Services were well attended, with 160 worshippers at the morning service and 302 present in the evening of 30 March 1851, in a building which could accommodate 500 worshippers.[171] Membership declined

---

156 Broad (ed.), *Bishop Wake's summary*, 735–6.
157 Lincs. Archives, DIOC/GIBSON/4, p. 18.
158 W.G.D. Fletcher, 'Documents relating to Leicestershire preserved in the Episcopal registers at Lincoln, part III', *Assoc. Archit. Soc. Rep. & Papers*, 22 (1893–4), 265.
159 R.H. Evans, 'Nonconformists in Leicestershire in 1669', *Trans. LAHS*, 25 (1949), 122; A Betteridge, 'Early Baptists in Leicestershire and Rutland III: General Baptists', *The Baptist Quarterly*, 25 (1973), 366.
160 Broad (ed.), *Bishop Wake's summary*, 736; Lincs. Archives, DIOC/GIBSON/4, p. 18.
161 Broad (ed.), *Bishop Wake's summary*, 736.
162 Fletcher, 'Documents relating to Leicestershire', 265.
163 P. Austin, 'Barton in the Beans', *The Baptist Quarterly*, 11 (1945), 420.
164 ROLLR, QS 44/2/8.
165 A. Betteridge, 'Barton-in-the-Beans Leicestershire: a source of church plants', *The Baptist Quarterly*, 36 (1995), 74.
166 Ex. inf. the late Mr. Alfred Seneschall; ROLLR, QS 44/2/86.
167 Tablet on building.
168 ROLLR, QS 95/2/1/68.
169 NHL, no. 1074134, Baptist Church, Bondgate: accessed 30 Apr. 2016.
170 Baptist minutes, Sept. 1839, in private ownership.
171 TNA, HO 129/444/1/15.

from 154 in 1881 to 113 in 1903.[172] The chapel closed in 2007, with services transferred to Orchard Community Primary School.[173] The chapel was sold and converted into a house in 2014.

Independents

Through the efforts of the Leicestershire Association of Independent Churches and Ministers, a large room in a former factory was fitted up for worship in 1837, and ministers from across the county led services, in rotation.[174] A chapel was built in 1840 (Fig. 13.), for 'Independents or Congregationalists', on land in Clapgun Street purchased by Richard Hemsley and George Dixon.[175] It could accommodate 285 worshippers. A vestry and school room were added, and there were plans for a minister's house alongside.[176] On census Sunday in 1851, 67 people attended the morning service and 142 were present in the evening.[177] There was a resident minister by 1855,[178] but this chapel appears for the last time in the Congregational Year Book of 1858–9.[179] The building was purchased by a local company for use as a lecture hall, chiefly in connection with the Temperance Movement,[180] and later became a Sailors' and Soldiers' Club.

Wesleyan Methodists

John Wesley visited the countess at Donington Park on four occasions in 1742 and 1743,[181] and preached in Castle Donington in 1764, 1772 and 1774.[182] The first Wesleyan Chapel was built in Apes (renamed Apiary) Gate in 1777.[183] It was pulled down in 1823 and a new chapel built on the same site,[184] at a cost of £1,000.[185] The congregation had 180 members in 1829.[186] The chapel was enlarged in 1839,[187] to give 292 free and 292 other sittings. On 30 March 1851, 211 people attended morning worship, and 402 attended in the evening.[188] The building was enlarged again in 1873.[189] Vicar Arthur Mammatt recorded in 1882 that of all the dissenting groups in Donington the Wesleyans were the most numerous, and

---

172 G.T. Rimmington, 'Baptist membership in rural Leicestershire, 1881–1914', *The Baptist Quarterly*, 37 (1998), 393.

173 http://castledoningtonbaptistchurch.snappages.com/home.htm (accessed 12 May 2014).

174 *Leic. Merc.*, 20 Jan. 1838, 3; 13 November 1838, 2; ROLLR, 1D 41/44/666.

175 ROLLR, DE 1363 N/C/64/1.

176 ROLLR, DE 1363 N/C/64/1; Ryder (1997), 43.

177 TNA, HO 129/444/I/12.

178 *P.O. Dir. Leics. and Rutl.* (1855), 25.

179 ROLLR, DE 1363 N/C/64/2.

180 *Derby Telegraph*, 17 Nov. 1860.

181 T. Jackson (ed.), *The Journal of the Rev. John Wesley, A.M.* (1903), I, 349, 358, 377, 384.

182 Ibid., III, 155, 431; IV, 9.

183 QS 44/2/88.

184 ROLLR, N/M/64/52 f. 2v.

185 W. White, *Dir. Leics. and Rutl.* (Sheffield, 1846), 339.

186 ROLLR, QS 95/2/1/68.

187 W. White, *Dir. Leics. and Rutl.* (Sheffield, 1863), 485.

188 TNA HO 129/444/1/13.

189 W. White *Dir. Leics. and Rutl.* (Sheffield, 1877), 183.

Figure 14 *Laying the foundation stones for the Wesleyan Methodist Church, May 1905.*

'have the most money'.[190] Land on Market Place was purchased for £1,030 in 1904,[191] and a replacement church, designed by A.E. Lambert of Nottingham, opened in 1906 (Figs 13 and 14).[192] Built in red brick with stone dressings, two towers, the taller with an octagonal stone spire, flank a seven-light window over double doors. Inside, the church has U-shaped galleries supported on iron columns, and the windows have Art Noveau-style stained glass.[193] The community has produced three well-known preachers: Dr Joseph Beaumont (1795–1855), Dr James Dixon (1788–1871) and B. Archibald Harrison (1883–1945); Dixon and Harrison were also presidents of the Methodist Conference.

Primitive Methodists

A Primitive Methodist Chapel is said to have been built on Little Hill Steps by Robert Cotton during the 1830s, but no records of this congregation have been found, and the chapel was not recorded on any contemporary map. [194]

190 Northants RO, ML 601.
191 Property deeds, in hands of the trustees.
192 Plaque inside chapel.
193 NHL, No. 1389142, Methodist Church, Market Place: accessed 30 Apr. 2015.
194 Ex inf. the late Mrs Lawrence White, a granddaughter of Robert Cotton.

Salvation Army

The Salvation Army met in Gospel Hall in 1887, and continued to be recorded in Castle Donington in 1895 and in 1928,[195] but little more is known about their presence.

Selina, Countess of Huntingdon

The 9th earl of Huntingdon (d. 1746) married Selina Shirley in 1728, the daughter of Earl Ferrers of Staunton Harold.[196] Selina converted to Methodism in the 1730s and offered John Wesley a base at Donington for his Midlands preaching.[197] With her encouragement, her servant David Taylor preached locally to farmers and labourers and inspired a group of converts to build a meeting house at Barton-in-the-Beans, which spawned groups in Leicestershire, Nottinghamshire and Derbyshire, and became the New Connnexion of General Baptists.[198] By 1744, the countess had begun to correspond with George Whitefield, and her beliefs shifted towards Calvinism. She established a training college for evangelical ministers and provided new chapels in fashionable towns. The secession of the Countess of Huntingdon's Connexion from the Anglican church came in 1777, following the establishment of a chapel in Spa Fields, London.[199] When the countess died in 1791, 64 chapels were formally associated with her Connexion.[200] By 1856, there were 109 chapels within the Countess of Huntingdon's Connexion (none in Castle Donington) and a further 182 in the New Connexion of General Baptists.[201]

Post-Reformation Catholicism

One Catholic was noted in 1767: Margaret, the wife of John Matson, aged about 30.[202] Fathers Cooke and Noble from Mount St Bernard's Abbey visited and addressed a crowd in the market place in 1847, but this appears to have been an isolated event.[203] Lord Donington of Donington Hall (d. 1895) came from a Lancashire Catholic family; he became an Anglican in the 1830s and brought up his children as Anglicans, but returned spiritually to Rome in 1892.[204] The manor was held in this period by the 7th earl Cowper, whose sister, Lady Amabel Kerr, inherited in 1905. She established a Catholic chapel and priest at Melbourne Hall, and in 1928 a mass centre from Melbourne opened in Castle Donington, using a room in the Moira Arms. In 1935 a small chapel was erected on Mount Pleasant, dedicated to St John Fisher. The growing congregation acquired

---

195 C.N. Wright, *Dir. Leics. and Rutl.* (Leicester, 1887–8), 374; *Kelly's Dir. Leics. and Rutl.* (1895), 50 and (1928), 58.
196 *Complete Peerage*, vi, 661.
197 *ODNB*, s.v. 'Hastings , Selina, countess of Huntingdon (1707–1791)', accessed 15 Jul. 2013.
198 M. Watts, *The Dissenters: from the Reformation to the French Revolution* (1978, Oxford, 2002), 454–5.
199 *ODNB*, s.v. 'Hastings , Selina, countess of Huntingdon (1707–1791)', accessed 15 Jul. 2013.
200 Watts, *The Dissenters*, 447–8, 400–1.
201 *Wesleyan-Methodist Mag.* (1856), 335.
202 Lincs. Archives, DISS 1A/17/10.
203 *Tablet*, 3 Apr. 1847, 6; 9 Apr. 1927, 22.
204 *Leic. Chron. and Leics. Merc.*, 8 Oct. 1892, 11.

and moved into the former school premises on Castle Hill in 1959. As the congregation continued to expand, thoughts turned to building a modern church. At the invitation of the Anglican church, Catholic masses were once again celebrated in the medieval church of St Edward between 1984 and 1992, while the old school building was demolished, money raised and the site redeveloped. The Roman Catholic Church of the Risen Lord opened on Castle Hill in 1992, in a red brick building designed by Peter Webley.[205]

Church of St Edward, King and Martyr

The church of St Edward, King and Martyr comprises a chancel, clerestoried nave with wide north and south aisles, south porch, and a west tower surmounted by a recessed needle spire (Figs 15 and 16). The predominant building material is local sandstone. The fabric is essentially of the 13th and early 14th centuries,[206] when the building was almost constantly altered and upgraded.

Three parts of the fabric predate the substantial building activity which took place from c.1200, and demonstrate that an earlier stone building stood on this site with a nave of the same length as its successor: the lowest stage of the west tower, with a single lancet window to the west and walls almost six feet thick, the nave walls between the east end of the arcades and the chancel arch, and the lower part of the chancel's north wall, where there are hints of a Romanesque arch extending under a tomb recess of the late 13th century.[207] The east end and its clasping buttresses appear to contain some reused stone.

A narrow south aisle of four bays was added in the early 13th century, and the bases of its circular piers are surrounded by stone seating. The chancel was refashioned at the same time, its piscina and triple sedilia on the south wall having similar 'water-holding' bases. The chancel at this time appears to have had three single-lancet windows in the north wall and four on the south, but only the two easternmost on the north and the centre two on the south are unaltered.

The north aisle is a little later but still Early English in style, perhaps built in the mid 13th century, and was originally narrower. The arcade has hexagonal piers, with stone seats at their base. Both arcades have a little dog-tooth decoration. The conversion of the assumed western lancet on the north wall of the chancel to a two-light window with quatrefoil may have taken place at about the same time.

Towards the end of the 13th century, the south aisle was widened along its whole length and a south chapel created, with a double piscina and two narrow sedilia at its eastern end. This is almost certainly St Mary's chapel, recorded in 1301.[208] Externally, the aisle is of five bays containing four windows each of two lights, bearing no relation to the internal piers. The chapel has an east window of three lights with trefoils, and outside the church, two of the buttresses have niches for statues. A squint provides a view of the chapel's altar from the west end of the chancel, its cusped lancet head suggesting

205 *Nottingham Dioc. Yearbk 1993*, 141–4.
206 Pevsner, 123.
207 This section is based on Pevsner, 123–4, Hamilton Thompson, 'An account', 78–86, NHL, no. 1361370, Church of St Edward, King and Martyr, accessed 21 May 2015, and personal observation. The plan is based on one by A. Herbert (1926) in Hamilton Thompson, 'An account'.
208 TNA, DL 25/1771.

Figure 15 *Church of St Edward, King and Martyr.*

Figure 16 *Development of St Edward's church.*

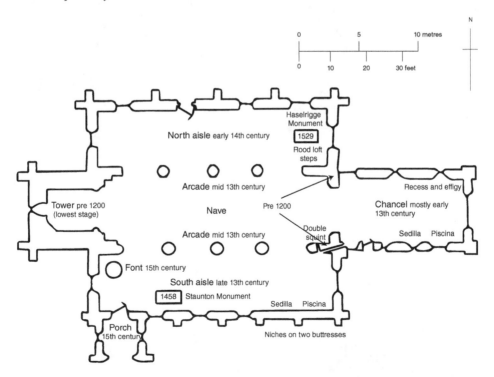

a late 13th-century date. A recess in the chancel's north wall is stylistically similar to the chapel's piscina, and may have been created at the same time, perhaps for the tomb of the first 'St Mary Priest', replacing whatever stood under the Romanesque arch. At about the same time the eastern lancet in the south wall of the chancel was converted to a two-light window with simple Y-tracery. The effigy of the priest is later, c.1320–30.

The upper stages of the tower and the spire were rebuilt in the late 13th or 14th century. The north aisle was widened in the early 14th century, perhaps to meet the needs of an expanding population, but this work was never completed: the hood moulds round the windows of the north aisle terminate in blocks of stone which still await the carver. This contrasts with those round the windows of the chancel and south aisle, which are finished with a carved head on each side, with the exception of that closest to the porch which may have been obstructed by an earlier porch. The north aisle is also the only part of the church which does not have a crenelated parapet.

A stair to the rood loft, at the east end of the north aisle, has no datable features. It commences about seven feet from the floor, and was presumably accessed by a wooden ladder. The clerestory was added in the 15th century, but the carved corbels which supported the earlier roof remain. The font was replaced in the 15th century, and the porch was added or rebuilt at that time. The western lancet in the chancel, near a priest's door, was converted to a square-headed low side window, probably in the late medieval period. A second squint was added to the first to provide a line of sight between the altar in the south chapel and the eastern part of the nave and part of the north chapel. It has no datable features but may relate to Harold Staunton's will of 1513, which established a daily mass commencing immediately after the high mass had been consecrated.[209]

209 TNA, PROB 11/17/257.

LOCAL GOVERNMENT

DONINGTON WAS ONLY EVER A SEIGNIORIAL borough. Burgesses are mentioned from 1311,[1] and 43 burgage plots were identified in 1462,[2] but the burgesses held their plots by customary tenure, and there is no evidence that they ever played a part in the management of the town's affairs. Manorial courts met regularly into the early 20th century. Vestry government was replaced by a parish council in 1894, which continued to meet in 2016.

Manor Courts and Officers

Manorial Government

Manor courts were held in a decayed house in the middle of the castle yard in 1564.[3] By the 19th century the venue had moved to the Moira Arms.[4] The court baron met at intervals of two to five weeks in 1458,[5] but by 1526 the frequency had reduced to every two months.[6] A court leet or view of frankpledge was held twice yearly at Easter and Michaelmas. The steward was said to have been paid to hold an annual court on Derby Hills, but no records of this survive, and it was claimed in 1554 that none had been held there for 16 years.[7] Annual perambulations of the bounds at Derby Hills by the manorial jury ceased in 1712.[8]

Between 1400 and 1628, the people of Donington also had direct access to the Court of Duchy Chamber, which could investigate claims and arbitrate when disagreements arose. Six cases were brought against steward Thomas Grey by the tenants between 1538 and 1565, for falsifying court rolls, preventing free election of manorial officers, making over copyholds to himself, taking timber and osiers, and overgrazing the commons.[9] Between 1565 and 1600, 26 cases against the tenants were brought by Grey's son, who

---

1   TNA, C 134/22/17.
2   TNA, DL 43/6/3; Farnham, 56–63.
3   TNA, DL 44/105.
4   For example, *Leic. Merc.*, 1 Nov. 1851, 3.
5   TNA, DL 30/80/90.
6   Melb. Hall Est. Office, X94/40/3.
7   TNA, DL 30/80/1100 m. 3.
8   Town bk, 1667; Melb. Hall Est. Office, X94/58/6/36.
9   TNA, DL 1/11/G1; DL 3/32/S1; DL 3/60/C2; DL 3/63/C3; DL 3/75/H1; DL 3/81/C4.

held no manorial office,[10] and 17 cases against him,[11] with 17 of the 43 cases involving either the Roby or Haselrigge family.

Customs

All copyholds were by inheritance.[12] Entry fines varied in the 16th century, partly due to apparent false accounting by the Duchy's steward Thomas Grey (I).[13] The entry fine was settled by decree in 1598 at a maximum of four years' rent,[14] but uncertainty followed a court decision in 1637 that this was not binding on a purchaser of the manor,[15] leading to the compounding of fines in the 1630s and 1640s.[16]

Perhaps to prevent future confusion, the customs of the manor were recited in 1661 and written up by the villagers in a town book. Copyholders could exchange land without any alteration of rent, borrow by mortgage for up to one year, agree leases for up to 21 years, cut down trees or gorse growing on their land for their own use, and take stone from common land to repair or maintain their property. All inhabitants could use Wilne ferry as often as they wished for an annual payment of 4d. for husbandmen and 1d. for cottagers,[17] and they could 'cleetch' [fish by hand, or with a shallow vessel] in the Trent and its pools with 'Cleeching netts', but not with rods, eel traps or larger nets to catch shoals.[18] Manorial incidents were gradually extinguished in the 1920s and 1930s.[19]

Officers

The office of constable passed annually between the occupants of certain houses in the 17th century, although they could find another person to perform the duties.[20] The custom resulted in women occasionally being liable to serve, and William Evatt performed the duties in 1672 for widow Ann Hibbard.[21] An additional constable was 'summoned' from the inhabitants of Derby Hills to serve for that area.[22] The constables' responsibilities encompassed law and order, collecting national taxes,[23] and repairing

---

10   TNA, DL 1/86/G4; DL 1/86/G8; DL 1/91/G3; DL 1/100/G2; DL 1/104/G3; DL 1/107/G6; DL 1/111/G7; DL 1/121/G12; DL 1/124/A35,DL 1/125/G7; DL 1/128/A43; DL 1/132/A38; DL 1/133/G7; DL 1/135/G5; DL 1/140/A6; DL 1/107/G6; DL 1/111/G7; DL 1/121/G12; DL 1/124/A35; DL 1/125/G7; DL 1/128/A43; DL 1/132/A38; DL 1/133/G7; DL 1/135/G5; DL 1/140/A6; DL 1/211/G1.

11   TNA, DL 1/81/A4; DL 1/83/R5; DL 1/88/W10; DL 1/89/23; DL 1/94/R6; DL 1/95/T11; DL 1/98/H9; DL 1/102/T3; DL 1/118/T5; DL 1/122/H5; DL 1/129/H3; DL 1/132/A17; DL 1/132/A35; DL 1/118/T5; DL 1/129/H3; DL 1/132/A17; DL 1/132/A35.

12   TNA, DL 43/6/5, f. 14.

13   TNA, DL 3/81/C4; DL 1/155/R6, 1/174/R7.

14   Melb. Hall Est. Office, X94/40/1/9; TNA, DL 43/6/5.

15   Melb. Hall Est. Office, X94/40/1/15.

16   Melb. Hall Est. Office, X94/40/1/16-20.

17   Town bk, 1661.

18   ROLLR, 4D 51/1, f. 66.

19   Melb. Hall Est. Office, X94/42/2.

20   Town bk, 1662, 1667, 1672.

21   Ibid., 1672.

22   Melb. Hall Est. Office, X94/58/5/28.

23   Town bk, 1659, 1689.

the archery butt, still present in 1644.[24] The strength of religious dissent in the late 17th century placed the constable at the centre of local tensions when illegal conventicles were held, or when people refused to pay their tithes. A fine of £5 was levied on the constable for not acting on information about a Quaker meeting in 1679, but later remitted, as neglect could not be shown.[25] The village had a set of stocks for those guilty of minor misdeeds,[26] and by the 19th century there was a lock-up on Castle Hill.[27] The role had then ceased to change hands regularly. Nathaniel Berrington served from 1805 for at least five years,[28] and James Newbold held the office for more than 26 years from the 1820s.[29]

Four field reeves were chosen each year whose duties included hiring an oxherd and neatherd to look after the cattle,[30] collecting the annual fee of 4*d*. from inhabitants holding 'groat pastures',[31] collecting rents from those living on Derby Hills,[32] paying for osiers to be set,[33] and trying to prevent flooding. In 1669 and 1670 they paid for 'waterworke stone' and gorse bundles to be put in the river in an attempt to control its course.[34]

Parish Government and Officers

Parish Government before 1894

From 1762, the manorial officers of constable and field reeve were chosen by the parish vestry.[35] The field reeves absorbed the duties of overseer of the highways until 1766, when separate accounts were produced for the two roles. From 1802, two people generally served for the highways for two years, stepping down in alternate years to ensure continuity.[36]

Two overseers of the poor were chosen each year.[37] Two annually elected churchwardens also had poor law duties until 1834, alongside responsibilities for the church,[38] including setting and collecting the church rate which was based, in the 17th century, on the number of pastures held and livestock owned.[39] Despite the strength of nonconformity in the village, this does not appear to have been contentious, perhaps

---

24   Melb. Hall Est. Office, X94/41/1.
25   ROLLR, 12D 39/34, ff. 2–3.
26   Town bk, 1684.
27   Photograph in B.M. Townsend, *Castle Donington in the Seventeenth Century: a Manorial Society* (Castle Donington, 1971), 34.
28   Town bk, from 1800.
29   ROLLR, QS 38/7; DE 5491/227.
30   Town bk, 1663, 1664, 1669, 1676.
31   Ibid., 1634.
32   Ibid., 1658, 1659.
33   Ibid., 1675.
34   Ibid., 1669, 1670.
35   Ibid., 1762.
36   Ibid., from 1800.
37   Above, 76–7.
38   Town bk, from 1800.
39   Ibid., 1634, 1659, 1664.

because levies were modest and infrequent, as the church received an income from land and houses.[40]

Burial Board

A burial board of nine members was formed in 1877, [41] but in 1879, with work to create a new cemetery within three weeks of completion, Mr Abney-Hastings of Donington Park lodged an objection to its location on Park Lane.[42] The board accepted his offer to cover the cost of relocating to a 4 a. site on Barroon and to provide £1,000 cash to reduce the parish rates.[43] The cemetery, with two chapels and a lodge, opened in 1881.[44] The duties of the burial board were transferred to the parish council in 1894.[45] The chapels were demolished in 1964, but the cemetery remained in use in 2016.[46]

Parish Government after 1894

Parish Council

The first parish council elections in 1894 attracted 21 candidates for the ten positions, and appeals to the electorate were made on party lines. S. Barrowdale, who had previously chaired vestry meetings, topped the poll, and was one of only three Liberals chosen. The council's first chairman was the vicar, Reverend Roney-Dougal, a Conservative.[47] Fierce party rivalry in 1904, when the Liberals won a majority of seats, led to an unseemly dispute about whether Mr Shields (Conservative) or Laurence Stevenson (a Liberal who had failed to be re-elected) was chairman.[48] The first female councillor was Miss Eaton, elected in 1928.[49]

The council had 14 members in 2015, who served on three committees: planning, recreation and amenities. In addition to providing services and supporting local organisations, a vital part of their work, especially from the 1970s, has been to provide input to the district council on planning matters, where the parish council stood between residents with concerns about the rapid erosion of green spaces in the parish, and commercial developers.[50]

---

40   Town bk, 1664, 1681, 1682.
41   *Kelly's Dir. Leics. and Rutl.* (1881), 503.
42   *Derby Daily Telegraph*, 23 Sept. 1879.
43   Ibid., 5 Nov 1879.
44   *Kelly's Dir. Leics. and Rutl.* (1891), 550.
45   *Kelly's Dir. Leics. and Rutl.* (1895), 50.
46   Castle Donington Local History Society, *More Memories of Castle Donington* (Castle Donington, 1986), 4; http://castledonington.leicestershireparishcouncils.org/cemetery.html (accessed 24 May 2016).
47   *Leic. Chron.*, 22 Dec. 1894; *Derby Daily Telegraph*, 9 Jan. 1895.
48   *Loughborough Monitor and News*, 28 Apr. 1904; 5 May 1904.
49   *Derby Daily Telegraph*, 24 Feb. 1928.
50   Annual report, 2010–11.

Policing

An Association for the Prosecution of Felons existed from at least 1811,[51] which covered the cost of prosecuting alleged criminals, and provided rewards for information resulting in conviction. It was sufficiently active to agree a new set of rules in 1856, and still met in 1888.[52] The village adopted the Lighting and Watching Act of 1833,[53] and was therefore excluded from police cover and from paying the police rate when a small county constabulary was formed in 1839.[54] Four or sometimes six watchmen were sent out each night, and 70–80 residents agreed to watch if there was ever a greater need.[55] Concerns were raised in 1841, when the chief constable sought to take Donington within the ambit of the county police,[56] and this was delayed until at least 1849.[57] An undated petition signed by 71 residents claimed they could not afford to maintain the watch if they paid the police rate, and would feel less secure unless two police officers were constantly stationed there.[58] A policeman was based in the village by 1853.[59] The police office in Borough Street closed in 2010,[60] but police surgeries continued to be held in the village in 2016.[61]

51   *Leic. Jnl*, 4 Jan. 1811.
52   ROLLR, DE 2111/1.
53   ROLLR, DE 5491/227.
54   *Leic. Merc.*, 18 Oct. 1839.
55   ROLLR, DE 5491/227.
56   *Leic. Merc.*, 27 Nov. 1841.
57   Ibid., 20 Oct. 1849.
58   ROLLR, DE 5491/227; QS 38/7.
59   *Notts Guardian*, 8 Sept. 1853.
60   http://www.derbytelegraph.co.uk/Village-police-offices-close-force-s-drive-cut-spending-163-15m/story-11574367-detail/story.html (accessed 15 Aug. 2015).
61   https://www.leics.police.uk/local-policing/valley (accessed 29 Jan. 2016).

Sources Used

THIS VCH HISTORY OF CASTLE DONINGTON has been written using a wide range of original documents, some of them printed, but mostly manuscript sources. It is that dependence on primary sources (i.e. created at the time under study) which makes VCH histories both new and reliable. This list includes the main sources used, but is not comprehensive. It should be used in conjunction with the footnotes and the List of Abbreviations. A very important resource is the website of The National Archives http://www.nationalarchives.gov.uk/, which gives access to detailed catalogues and research guides, as well as references to a selection of material held in other record repositories around the country.

Manuscript Sources

Public Repositories

The National Archives (TNA) at Kew holds the records of national government from the late 12th century onwards, with some earlier material. Calendars (brief abstracts) of some of the administrative records of government in the middle ages and early modern period have been published, and have also been used in this history. TNA also holds the records of the duchy of Lancaster, a major landowner in Castle Donington for over 200 years. The main classes of manuscript documents used in this history are:

BN 62	Home Office Children's Department, 1897–1990
C 134	Chancery inquisitions post mortem, 1307–27
C 135	Chancery inquisitions post mortem, 1327–77
DL 1	Duchy of Lancaster, Court of Duchy Chamber, pleadings, 1485–1628
DL 3	Duchy of Lancaster, Court of Duchy Chamber, pleadings, depositions and examinations 1485–1558
DL 4	Duchy of Lancaster, Court of Duchy Chamber, pleadings, depositions and examinations, 1558–1628
DL 25	Duchy of Lancaster, deeds
DL 28	Duchy of Lancaster, accounts, 1400–1628
DL 29	Duchy of Lancaster, accounts, 1400–1628
DL 30	Duchy of Lancaster, court rolls, 1400–1628
DL 42	Duchy of Lancaster, cartularies, enrolments and surveys, 1400–1628

DL 43	Duchy of Lancaster, rentals and surveys, 1400–1628
DL 44	Duchy of Lancaster, special commissions, 1558–1628
E 179	Exchequer taxation records, 1190–1690
E 182	Exchequer land taxes, 1689–1830
ED 2	Elementary Education, parish files, 1872–1904
ED 21	Public Elementary School, files, 1857–1946
ED 103	Privy Council on Education, building grants, 1833–81
HO 107	Home Office, Census Enumerators' Returns, 1841, 1851
HO 129	Home Office, Ecclesiastical Census, 1851
IR 18	Tithe Files, 1836–70
MAF 32	National Farm Survey Farm Records, 1941–43
MAF 68	Agricultural Returns, 1866–1988
MAF 140	Ministry of Agriculture, land acquisition by other government departments, 1941–71
MH 12	Correspondence of Poor Law Commissioners, Shardlow Union, 1833–1900
PROB 11	Probate records, Prerogative Court of Canterbury, to 1858
RG 9	General Register Office, Census Enumerators' returns, 1861–1911
SC 6	Ministers' and receivers' accounts
TS 11	Treasury solicitors' papers
WO 30	War Office miscellaneous papers

The Record Office for Leicestershire, Leicester and Rutland (ROLLR) in Wigston, Leicestershire holds records of county administration, records of the diocese of Leicester (from 1926), some earlier archidiaconal records, and numerous parish, school and private records. The principal classes of documents used in this history are:

14D 32	Hastings letters
5D 33	Farnham bequest
12D 39	Quaker records
1D 41	Leicester Archdeaconry records (includes class 1850'245)
6D 45	Turnpike books
4D 51	Roby Family papers
7D 53	Rentals
32D 73	Leicester Water Department Records
DE 253	Enclosure papers
DE 1168 (N/M/64)	Methodist Church records
DE 1177	National Coal Board documents
DE 1363	Leicestershire and Rutland Congregational Union records
DE 1524	NorthWest Leicestershire and predecessor District Council minutes

DE 2072	Duties on Land Values records
DE 2111	Castle Donington Association for the Prosecution of Felons
DE 3115	Charities Trust records
DE 4365	Castle Donington High School deposit
DE 5251	Enclosure papers
DE 5491	Leicestershire Constabulary records
DE 5569	Castle Donington St Edward's School records
DE 8371	Castle Donington Independent Friendly Society records
DG 8	Genealogical Society Collection, Walton and Vincent family papers
DG 9	Herrick papers
DG 30	Crane and Walton deposit, includes classes 4D 42, DE 362 and DE 500
OS	Ordnance Survey maps
	Parish registers
PR/I	Leicester Archdeaconry probate records, 1542–1812
QS 38	Quarter Sessions petitions and memoranda
QS 44	Quarter Sessions Licences for Protestant Dissenters' meeting houses
QS 62	Quarter Sessions Land Tax Assessments
QS 75	Quarter Sessions Deposited plans for gas undertakings
QS 95	Quarter Sessions licences for teachers and meeting houses
	Will and Inventory files, Leicester Archdeaconry, 1500–1603
	Will registers, Leicester Archdeaconry, 1515–33
	Will files, Leicester Archdeaconry, 1563–1858

Castle Donington Museum Trust holds a number of original records relating to Castle Donington, including school and friendly society records, and family papers.

Derbyshire Record Office in Matlock holds family estate papers for the Barons Donington (D1336), the Harpur Crewe family (D2375) and the Holden family (D779), which contain significant information about Castle Donington. The Cavendish Bridge Trust records (D533) and deposits of enclosure maps and awards with the Derbyshire quarter sessions (Q/RI) are also relevant.

Huntington Library, San Marino, California holds many records relating to the Hastings family, who owned Donington Park for over 300 years. The following classes of documents have been used:

Hastings Deposit, HAD Hastings deeds

Hastings Deposit, HAF 15 Hastings accounts and financial papers, 1640–44

Hastings Deposit, HAL 11 Hastings legal papers, 1650–70

Hastings Deposit, HAM 8 Hastings manorial papers, Castle Donington, 1439–1777

Hastings Deposit, HAM 9 Hastings manorial papers, Castle Donington, 1778–1815

Hastings Deposit, Misc 8 Castle Donington Churchwardens' accounts

Lambeth Palace Library in Lambeth and the **Church of England Records Centre** in South Bermondsey hold central records of the Church of England, including records of the Incorporated Church Building Society, the augmentation of livings and records relating to National (Church of England) schools.

Lincolnshire Archives holds records relating to the Diocese of Lincoln, which included Castle Donington until 1837. The most important classes used are the glebe terriers (surveys of land belonging to the church) and microfilm copies of the visitations of Bishop Gibson (1718-21).

Northamptonshire Record Office holds visitation records relating to the parish church between 1837 and 1926, when Castle Donington was within the Diocese of Peterborough.

Nottinghamshire Archives holds a medieval account for Castle Donington manor (DD/FJ/6) and Quaker records which include Castle Donington (NC/Q/208).

Private Archives

Castle Donington Church holds the Town Book, which includes entries detailing many different aspects of everyday life from the 17th to the 19th century.

Melbourne Hall Estate Office holds the private archive of the Coke family, lords of the manor of Castle Donington from 1633 (Lothian Collection). This includes:

X94/37	Manor court leases and enfranchisements
X94/39	Indentures and deeds
X94/40	Ownership and customs of manor, manorial accounts (1392–1404), court rolls (1462–1558) and surveys
X94/41	Manor court rolls 1644–1759
X94/42	Manor court books 1822–1944
X94/52	Surveys and valuations
X94/57	Trent navigation, commerce and industry
X94/58	Dispute over Derby Hills land
X94/P/1	Maps of Derby Hills

Printed Sources

Primary Sources

The most important printed sources, including calendars of major classes of records in The National Archives and parliamentary papers, are included in the List of Abbreviations. The Lincoln Record Society has published many original records of the ancient diocese of Lincoln which contain information about Castle Donington, and transcripts of other original documents can be found in the *Associated Architectural*

Societies, Reports and Papers. Good collections of Leicestershire trade directories are held at ROLLR.

National newspapers and local newspapers from Leicestershire, Derbyshire and Nottinghamshire have also been used extensively in this research.

Books and Articles

John Nichols' *History and Antiquities of the County of Leicester* remains an important secondary source for the history of the county, and the Castle Donington entry is in volume III (1804). It largely incorporates the earlier *Description of Leicestershire* by William Burton (1622). Nichols added original copies of the sketches and paintings used in his engravings within his own copies of the volumes, and this 'grangerised' set is held at ROLLR. An invaluable guide to the Duchy and its records is R. Somerville's, *History of the Duchy of Lancaster.* Historian George Farnham published transcripts of many records in G.F. Farnham and A. Hamilton Thompson, 'The castle and manor of Castle Donington, with an account of the church', *Transactions of the Leicestershire Archaeological and Historical Society*, 14 (1925–6). These transcriptions have been checked against the original documents, and a number of errors and omissions have been discovered. The references in this history are therefore to the original documents at TNA.

The main sources used for architectural history are N. Pevsner (rev. E. Williamson), *The Buildings of England; Leicestershire and Rutland* (2nd edn, Harmondsworth, 1984), the various listings of properties on the Heritage List for England, and two historic buildings appraisals by P.F. Ryder, shown in the List of Abbreviations, copies of which are held by the Historic Environment team at Leicestershire County Hall.

Assoc. Archit. Soc. Rep. & Papers	*Associated Architectural Societies, Reports and Papers*
Burton	W. Burton, *The Description of Leicestershire* (2nd edn, 1777)
CADMT	Castle Donington Museum Trust
Cal. Close	*Calendar of the Close Rolls*
Cal. Inq. p.m.	*Calendar of Inquisitions Post Mortem*
Cal. Pat.	*Calendar of the Patent Rolls*
Cal. SP Dom.	*Calendar of State Papers, Domestic*
Calamy Revised	A.G. Matthews, *Calamy Revised being a revision of Edmund Calamy's Account of the Ministers and Other Ejected and Silenced, 1660–2* (Oxford, 1934)
Cart. Chester, I	J. Tait (ed.), *The Chartulary or Register of the Abbey of St Werburgh, Chester*, part I (Chetham Society, n.s. 79, Manchester, 1920)
Cart. Chester, II	J. Tait (ed.), *The Chartulary or Register of the Abbey of St Werburgh, Chester*, part II (Chetham Society, n.s. 82, Manchester, 1923)
CDPC	Castle Donington Parish Council
CJ	*Journals of the House of Commons*
Complete Peerage	V. Gibbs, H.A. Doubleday and Lord Howard de Walden (eds.), *The Complete Peerage of England, Scotland, Ireland, Great Britain and the United Kingdom* (1910–38)
Cooper and Ripper	L.P. Cooper and S. Ripper, 'A medieval manorial fishery at Hemington Quarry, Castle Donington', University of Leicester Archaeological Services, ULAS report 2012-023 (Leicester, 2012)
Derb. Merc.	*Derby Mercury*
Domesday	A. Williams and G.H. Martin (eds), *Domesday Book: A Complete Translation* (2002)
Derb. RO	Derbyshire Record Office

Farnham   G.F. Farnham and A. Hamilton Thompson, 'The castle
                                 and manor of Castle Donington, with an account of the
                                 church', *Transactions of the Leicestershire Archaeological
                                 and Historical Society*, xiv (1925–6)

Fox   L. Fox, 'Ministers' accounts of the Honor of Leicester
                                 (1322–1324)', *Trans. LAHS*, xix (1936–7), 209–11, 240–73.

HC Deb.   *Parliamentary Debates, House of Commons*

HL Deb.   *Parliamentary Debates, House of Lords*

HMC   *Historical Manuscripts Commission*

Huntington Libr.   Huntington Library, San Marino, California, Hastings
                                 collection

L & P Henry VIII   *Letters and Papers of Henry VIII*

Leics. & Rutl. HER   Historic Environment Record for Leicestershire and
                                 Rutland

Leics. CC Planning Dept.   Leicestershire County Council Planning Department

Leic. Chron.   *Leicester Chronicle*

Leic. Chron. and Leics.   *Leicester Chronicle and Leicestershire Mercury*
Merc.

Leic. Jnl   *Leicester Journal*

Leics. Merc.   *Leicestershire Mercury*

Melb. Hall Est. Office   Melbourne Hall Estate Office

NHL   National Heritage List for England
                                 http://www.historicengland.org.uk/listing/the-list

Nichols   J. Nichols, *History and Antiquities of the County of Leicester*
                                 (1795–1815)

OS   Ordnance Survey

Parl. Papers   Parliamentary papers

Pevsner   N. Pevsner (rev. E. Williamson), *The Buildings of England;
                                 Leicestershire and Rutland* (2nd edn, Harmondsworth,
                                 1984)

Poll Taxes 1377–81, (ed.)   C.C. Fenwick (ed.), *Poll Taxes of 1377, 1379 and 1381*, pt 1
Fenwick   (British Academy Records of Social and Economic Hist.
                                 n.s. 27, 1998); pt 2 (n.s. 29, 2001)

Ripper and Cooper   S. Ripper and L.P. Cooper, *The Hemington Bridges: the
                                 excavation of three medieval bridges at Hemington Quarry,
                                 near Castle Donington, Leicestershire* (Leicester, 2009)

ROLLR   Record Office for Leicestershire, Leicester and Rutland

Ryder (1997)   P.F. Ryder, 'Castle Donington: A Historic Buildings
                                 Appraisal' (1997)

Ryder (2000)	P.F. Ryder, 'Castle Donington: A Historic Buildings Appraisal – High Street' (2000)
Somerville, *History*	R. Somerville, *History of the Duchy of Lancaster*, 2 vols (1953 and 1970)
Tax. Eccl.	*Taxatio Ecclesiastica Anglie et Wallie ... circa AD 1291* (Record Commission, 1801)
TNA	The National Archives
Trans. LAHS	*Transactions of the Leicestershire Archaeological and Historical Society*
Valor Eccl.	*Valor Ecclesiasticus, temp. Hen. VIII* (Record Commission, 1810–34)

GLOSSARY

The following technical terms may require explanation. Fuller information on local history topics is available in D. Hey, *The Oxford Companion to Local and Family History* (1996), or online at the VCH website (http://www.victoriacountyhistory.ac.uk). The most convenient glossary of architectural terms is Pevsner's Architectural Glossary (2010), also available for iPhone and iPad.

Advowson: the right to nominate a candidate to the bishop for appointment as rector or vicar of a church. This right was a form of property which was often attached to a manor, but could be bought and sold.

Amercement: the fine for an offence at a manorial court leet (q.v.).

Anglo-Saxon: A period of English history from 410–1066 AD, divided into early Anglo-Saxon (410–650 AD) and late Anglo-Saxon (650–1066 AD).

Attainder: an order made by a judge or Act of Parliament by which the real and personal estate of a convicted individual was forfeited and could not be inherited.

Bailiff: (1) the holder of a public office in certain districts; (2) the agent of the lord of the manor, responsible for administering the estate and collecting the rents.

Bailiwick: a place or district under the jurisdiction of a bailiff (q.v.).

Beaker: a wide-mouthed drinking vessel found in the graves of a people who came to Britain from central Europe in the early Bronze Age (q.v.).

Black Death: the name given to a European pandemic of the mid 14th century with high levels of mortality, generally believed to be bubonic plague, which reached England in 1348.

Bobbin net: A type of machine-made fine lace netting (tulle) created by looping the weft thread diagonally around the warp to form a hexagonal mesh.

Bordar: a smallholder, farming land recently brought into cultivation on the edge of a settlement.

Borough: a town either with its own government granted by royal charter, or one with a lesser degree of independence from the manorial lord, where the burgesses (q.v.) could administer the town's affairs through an institution such as a guild (q.v.).

Bovate: one-eighth of a carucate (q.v.), varying from *c.*10–18 a.

Bronze Age: A period of English history from 2500–800 BC, divided into early Bronze Age (2500–1500 BC), middle Bronze Age (1500–1000 BC) and late Bronze Age (1000–800 BC).

Burgage: a plot of land fronting a market place or main street in a town, characteristically long and thin in shape, occupied by a burgess (q.v.), usually for a money rent (burgage tenure).

Burgess: a citizen of a borough, often a member of its governing body.

Burnt mound: an archaeological feature comprising a mound of shattered stones and burnt charcoal from the Neolithic (q.v.) or Bronze Age (q.v.).

Carucate: originally the amount of land a team of eight oxen could plough in a year. This could vary according to the quality of the land, but was typically *c.*120 a. Also called a ploughland.

Chantry: masses celebrated for the souls of the founder and anyone nominated by the founder, or for the souls of members of a guild (q.v.) or fraternity.

Classis: a governing body of pastors or elders in a non-episcopal church (one without bishops).

Commons: areas of land governed by agreements made at the manorial court, giving specified rights (e.g. of grazing a certain number of animals, or collecting furze) to certain people (e.g. the occupiers of ancient cottages).

Conventicle: a meeting of religious dissenters.

Copyhold: form of land tenure granted in a manor court, so called because the tenant received a 'copy' of the grant as noted in the court records.

Cottars: the lowest class of peasant, occupying just a cottage.

Court Baron: a local manorial court which dealt with transfers of copyhold land on inheritance or sale. It was usually held every three weeks.

Court of Duchy Chamber: a court based in London with jurisdiction over cases concerning the lands and revenues of the Duchy of Lancaster (q.v.) where the law did not provide adequate remedy.

Court Leet: a local manorial court which dealt with petty law and order and the regulation of agriculture, normally held every six months.

Customary tenure: unfree or copyhold tenure, regulated by local manorial custom.

Demesne: in the Middle Ages, land farmed directly by a lord of the manor, rather than granted to tenants. Although usually leased out from the later Middle Ages, demesne lands often remained distinct from the rest of a parish's land.

Duchy of Lancaster: a private estate owned by the Duke of Lancaster, including land in many English and Welsh counties. Since 1399, the Duke of Lancaster has been the reigning monarch, but the estate is kept separately from other Crown properties.

Feoffees: trustees appointed to manage land or other assets for the benefit of others.

First fruits and tenths: taxes paid by clergy, originally to Rome, equating to the first year's profits, followed by one-tenth of the assessed value of the benefice in future years.

Free tenant: a tenant who did not owe services to the lord of the manor.

Furlong: a block of strips in the open fields (q.v.).

Guild: a religious organisation offering mutual charitable support to its members, who might all have a common occupation. In some small towns the guild might administer the affairs of the town.

Glebe: land belonging to the church to support a priest.

Grange: a monastic farming complex, usually on land which was remote from the monastery.

Hearth tax: tax levied twice a year between 1662 and 1688, assessed on the number of hearths or fireplaces in a house.

Hospital: originally a charitable foundation for housing the elderly and infirm, as well as the sick. Often established as a form of chantry (q.v.) whose residents were required to pray for the soul of the founder.

Husbandman: a farmer who generally held his land by copyhold or leasehold tenure.

Impropriator: layman entitled to church lands or profits, for example those formerly belonging to a monastery dissolved at the Reformation.

Inclosure: the process whereby open fields was divided into fields, to be redistributed among the various tenants and landholders. From the 18th century, inclosure was usually by an Act of Parliament obtained by the dominant landowners; earlier, more commonly done by private agreement, or by a powerful lord acting on his own initiative.

Indult: a licence or permission granted by the Pope.

Iron Age: A period of English history from 800 BC–42 AD, divided into early Iron Age (800–100 BC) and late Iron Age (100 BC–42 AD).

Knight's fee or service: an amount of land capable of providing enough money to provide a knight for a set period of time – almost invariably 40 days – when required, though some fees demanded other kinds of military service, such as an archer or warhorse. Such obligations became monetary or in kind, and by the 13th century, as estates were divided up, smaller estates could be held as fractions of a knight's fee.

Lay subsidy: tax paid by the laity, raised for a specific purpose.

Lollard: a name given to followers of John Wyclif (c.1325–84) in his opposition to the established church. Lollards rejected priestly authority and advocated the study of scriptures in the vernacular.

Manor: a piece of landed property with tenants regulated by a private (manor) court. Originally held by feudal tenure (see knight's fee), manors descended through a succession of heirs, but could also be given away or sold.

Mark: unit of accounting, worth two-thirds of a pound.

Messuage: a house with its surrounding land and outbuildings.

Modus: the conversion of a tithe payment in kind to a fixed annual sum of money.

Neolithic: A period of English history from 4000–2500 BC. The period from 3000–2500 BC is generally referred to as late Neolithic.

Open (common) fields: communal agrarian organization under which an individual's farmland was held in strips scattered amongst two or more large fields, intermingled with the strips of other tenants. Management of the fields, and usually common meadows and pasture, was regulated through the manor court or other communal assembly.

Pale: a fence of vertical stakes around a deer park, often accompanied by a substantial earth bank.

Paleochannel: an old course of a river containing sediment, and sometimes water which no longer flows.

Pannage: the right to graze pigs on acorns and beech mast on commons (q.v.).

Parish: the area attached to a parish church and owing tithes to it. From the Elizabethan period it had civil responsibilities, hence a 'civil' as opposed to an 'ecclesiastical' parish. At first the two were usually identical, but from the 19th century, when many parishes were reorganized, their boundaries sometimes diverged.

Ploughland: another name for the carucate (q.v.).

Quitclaim: a document which performs or confirms the giving up of all claims to a piece of property.

Rectory: (1) a church living served by a rector, who generally received the church's whole income; (2) the church's property or endowment, comprising tithes, offerings and usually some land or glebe.

Recusant: a person who did not attend the services of the Church of England, as required by law, often (but not always) a Roman Catholic.

Roman: A period of English history from 42–410 AD, divided into early Roman (42–250 AD) and late Roman (250–410 AD).

Seigniorial borough: a borough (q.v.) belonging to a lord.

Selion: a strip of arable land in an open field.

Sokeman: a type of free peasant.

Stint: the number of animals a tenant was allowed to graze on common pastures, as agreed and enforced through the manor court.

Suit of court: a tenant's obligation to attend the lord's manor court.

Terrier: register of the lands belonging to a landowner, originally including a list of tenants, their holdings, and the rents paid, later consisting of a description of the acreage and boundaries of the property.

Tithe: a tax of one-tenth of the produce of the land, which originally went to the church. It could be divided into great tithes (corn and hay), which went to the rector, and small tithes (livestock, wool and other crops), which supported a vicar.

Transhumance: the practice of moving livestock from sheltered winter grazing to upland or woodland grazing for the summer months.

Turnpike: a road administered by a trust, which covered the cost of maintenance by charging tolls.

Vestry: (1) room in a church where clerical vestments are stored; (2) assembly of leading parishioners and ratepayers, responsible for poor relief and other secular matters as well as church affairs.

Vicar: originally a clergyman appointed to act as priest of a parish, particularly as assistant to or substitute for the rector. He received a stipend or a proportion of the church's income, such as the small tithes (q.v.).

Villan: the unfree tenant of a manorial lord, holding more land than other classes of unfree peasants.

Virgate: a standard holding of arable land in the Middle Ages, of quarter of a carucate, generally 15–40 a. depending on the quality of the land. A virgate usually generated surplus crops for sale at market; those with fractions of a virgate probably needed to work part-time for better-off neighbours. Also called a yardland.

Warp Blonde: A type of machine-knitted lace made from two interlocking threads of silk, which will ladder if damaged, but will not unravel.

Yardland: see virgate.

Yeoman: from the 16th century, a term used for larger and more prosperous farmers, sometimes owning freehold land, many of them socially aspirational.

INDEX

CPSIA information can be obtained
at www.ICGtesting.com
Printed in the USA
FSHW020535310321
79947FS